Vijay Tendulkar

A Pioneer Playwright

Vijay Tendulkar

A Pioneer Playwright

Shailaja B. Wadikar

ATLANTIC

PUBLISHERS & DISTRIBUTORS (P) LTD

Published by

ATLANTIC

PUBLISHERS & DISTRIBUTORS (P) LTD

7/22, Ansari Road, Darya Ganj,
New Delhi-110002
Phones : +91-11-40775252, 23273880, 23275880, 23280451
Fax : +91-11-23285873
Web : www.atlanticbooks.com
E-mail : orders@atlanticbooks.com

Branch Office
5, Nallathambi Street, Wallajah Road,
Chennai-600002
Phones : +91-44-64611085, 32413319
E-mail : chennai@atlanticbooks.com

Printed in India at Nice Printing Press, A-33/3A, Site-IV, Industrial Area, Sahibabad, Ghaziabad, U.P.

Dedicated to

The Everlasting Memory of

The Great Humanist

VIJAY TENDULKAR

FOREWORD

It is neither the study of author nor of author's series; it is a document revealing the reign of ruler renowned in the region of Indian Theatre and beyond boundaries too! Writings of Tendulkar mean difficult dilemma; though so, dimensions so glittering as in a diamond are very much different, perhaps because the writer is original as well as, what creation needs, indifferent in the sense of being aloof so as to be alert always. It can be said that Tendulkar as a believer and as beyond belief is a master of magnet beneath the earth. Dr. Shailaja has touched both the poles—profound and polemic!

Theatre never rests with single territory. World is the way; footprints of genuine traveler in any trans are considered to be parallel to milestones. Tendulkar proved it. Dr. Shailaja aims at showing the soul of silence a genius respires whenever it bursts "Court is in Session". Dr. Shailaja worked not for the thought but for thinking as thinking touches sensibility. Depicting as if myth, she exposed the reality. Tendulkar, a great sage of sensibility, evoked endless equations. The present work of Dr. Shailaja is a great witness of the same spirit!

Prof. Famu Shinde
Chairman
Stage Performances Scrutiny Board,
Govt. of Maharashtra, Mumbai.

ACKNOWLEDGEMENTS

At the very outset, I express my deep sense of gratitude to Dr. L.S. Deshpande, for initiating me into undertaking this work and also for his constant encouragement and insightful guidance in the study.

I am immensely indebted to all those erudite scholars who spared their valuable time in clearing my doubts and helping me sort out certain issues and present ideas on proper lines. The foremost among them is Dr. Bhalachandra Nemade (Mumbai) while others include Dr. Chandrashekhar Jahagirdar (Kolhapur), Prof. Ravindra Kimbahune (Aurangabad), Dr. Maya Pandit (Hyderabad), Vishwas Sahastrabuddhe (Pune), Dr. Padmakar Dadegaonkar (Hyderabad), Dr. N.M. Aston (Pune), and Prof. Pratap Dharamsi (Nanded). I am also indebted to Arundhati Banerjee, Manchi Sarat Babu, and Asha S. Kanwar for their invaluable critical study material on Tendulkar's plays.

My sincere thanks are due to the librarians of The English and Foreign Languages University, Hyderabad; Jaikar Library, Pune; Mumbai Marathi Granthsangrahalaya, Mumbai; Dr. Babasaheb Ambedkar Marathwada University, Aurangabad; Yeshwant Mahavidyalaya, Nanded; People's College, Nanded; and Swami Ramanand Teerth Marathwada University, Nanded. I would like to extend my special thanks to Mrs. Usha Kulkarni and Mrs. Neema Newasekar, librarians of Pratibha-Niketan College, Nanded and Dr. B.S. Varma of People's

College, Nanded for supplying me with reference books, journals, and some rare material on Tendulkar's plays.

My heartfelt gratitude to Ms. Sonali Kulkarni, S.R.T.M. University, Nanded, for making Internet services available.

I have no words to express my heartfelt gratitude to Prof. F.M. Shinde, Mrs. Leela Shinde, Dr. Saheb Khandare, Dr. Dhananjay Yedekar, Dr. Baburao Solunke, Dr. Sheshrao Suryavanshi, Dr. Nagnath Kotpalle, for aiding me in one way or another in completing this work.

I owe a great debt of gratitude to the members of my family, particularly my parents, for their constant help, encouragement, and cooperation.

Shailaja B. Wadikar

PREFACE

Vijay Tendulkar has been in the vanguard of the Indian Theatre for nearly five decades. His play *Silence! The Court is in Session* won him a place among the leading Indian playwrights and his *Ghashiram Kotwal* made a room for him in the international galaxy of the literati.

The Tendulkar drama highlights the complexity of human relationships and contains a latent critique of modern Indian society. Tendulkar's plays like Shakespeare's plays are neither moral, nor immoral in tone but may rather be seen as amoral.

The corpus of works under study consists of the translated plays of Tendulkar such as *Silence! The Court is in Session (Shantata! Court Chalu Ahe), The Vultures (Gidhade), Sakharam Binder, Ghashiram Kotwal, Encounter in Umbugland (Dambdwipcha Mukabala), Kamala, Kanyadan,* and *A Friend's Story (Mitrachi Goshta)*. Each of them reflects contemporary Indian society, its problems, and its challenges. However, most of them deal with the issues of the white-collar middle-class people. These plays give the audience a new awareness of truth which is difficult to encounter. In the playwright's deft handling of the complex and varied issues, one can clearly notice his keen observation of life. All the major aspects of life—psychological, socio-political, deterministic, existential, feminist, and humanitarian—are delineated in a realistic manner. The approach of thc dramatist in the depiction of the problematic nature of Indian society is a revolutionary one.

The dramatic movement in the western countries during the post-war period marks a definite break with the earlier

European drama. Instead of presenting sentimental love scenes, the dramatists like Ibsen, Shaw, Galsworthy, etc. have brought on stage social realism and prescribed truth to life. John Osborne's play *Look Back in Anger* depicts the contemporary English society and gives release to the anger and cruelty of the post-war young generation that ultimately lead them to the state of frustration.

In the post-independence Indian theatre, this feeling of pessimism is noticed in the dramatic works of Vijay Tendulkar, Girish Karnad, Mohan Rakesh, and Badal Sircar. All these four major dramatists present the problems of the day-to-day life. Among them, Tendulkar has been recognized as the leading playwright of the *avant-garde* movement in the Indian context.

Tendulkar's plays bring a turning point in Indian theatre as they shock the sensibility of the conventional audience by projecting the reality of life, human relationship, and existence. His plays are revolutionary in the sense that they bring about a transformation in the audience's mindset. They depict the doomed or "lost generation" of the post-independence India, where people are victims of wilful monstrosity.

In Tendulkar's plays, one can clearly notice his candid scrutiny of life. Majority of his plays are based on real-life events and incidents that Tendulkar himself has witnessed. The characters in the plays are the victims of hostile situations or harsh circumstances. The characters, either tender-hearted or aggressive, are the victims of chance, fate or circumstances. The suffering that they face reveals the deterministic overtones in their lives. They have to follow the law of life. The playwright's mute sympathy goes with these victims. In the treatment of his theme and delineation of characters, Tendulkar is outrightly a humanitarian, but, for that, one has to read his plays between the lines. Even "silence" in the places with "pauses" is eloquent.

The plays expose such vices of the society as hypocrisy, vulgarity, barbarism, corruption, narrow-mindedness, etc. In his attack on the society, the playwright's mutiny against the feudal values and his demand for the new code of conduct and morality are clearly perceptible.

Tendulkar's plays explore the depths of human mind. The themes of most of the plays under discussion except *Encounter in Umbugland* are related to love, sex and violence. The protagonists of the plays appear to be the spokesmen of the angry and frustrated post-independence generation. The plays, while portraying complexity of human nature, throw light on the shifts and changes in human attitudes. The language, the setting, the stage directions, etc. are in harmony with the situations and atmosphere of the plays. Symbolic elements are used on a large scale to reflect the characters' state of mind. In the portrayal of society, Tendulkar's plays mark a definite departure from the previous Marathi theatre. One of the reasons of people's strong reaction against his plays is their burning naturalism. Life here is projected with all its ugliness and crudity. It shocks the sensibility of the conventional readers. Such a direct confrontation with the vulgar reality is beyond the boundaries of their expectations.

Tendulkar is interested in showing disharmony rather than harmony in the relationship between man and society. There are tensions depicted in his plays—the tensions between individual identity and social existence. While exposing the vices and weaknesses of society and individuals, he remains a detached observer. However, one can notice his compassion for the victims of circumstances. Because of his realistic approach, he is far from being a shallow, hollow, and cheap entertainer. He depicts the filth and squalor he sees in the society around, with a desire to make people conscious of the problems and to make them think of their probable solutions. Who can be happier than Tendulkar, if people change and along with them, the society too changes?

Generally speaking, the life portrayed in Tendulkar's plays is sad, miserable and full of contradictions. But it is real. The anger and frustration of the protagonist are not without any reasons. The plays are thought-provoking and make the audience sensitive to the issues. Towards the end of the play's performance is seen the beginning of the audience's consciousness. They leave the theatre with their minds shocked or perturbed. Therefore, one notices Tendulkar dramatizing man's confrontation with reality. A Tendulkar play can be seen as a projection of the playwright's commitment to the values of life. The only thing that he aspires to is, in his own words, that "the show must go on". It, at once, sounds a dual note: his satire and his optimism.

The book presents real-life situations mirrored in Tendulkar's plays in a lucid manner and throws light on the complexity of human relationships as experienced by his characters. References have been provided to enable the readers to trace different sources and pursue an extensive study on Tendulkar. Appendix, which provides an interesting face-to-face with this eminent playwright, and Bibliography further enrich the book while Index helps in easy location of pertinent topics discussed within chapters.

It will prove highly useful to the students and teachers of Indian English Literature and Indian Theatre and researchers in these fields.

Shailaja B. Wadikar

CONTENTS

VANGUARD

1

The first Marathi playwright who has transformed the regional theatre into the national theatre is Tendulkar. So, Arundhati Banerjee is justified in saying: "Vijay Tendulkar has been in the vanguard of not just Marathi but Indian theatre for almost forty years."[1] Witnessing his plays, enacted on the stage by various countrywide theatre groups, the audience has an exposure to the country's national theatre and its rich and varied dramaturgical legacy and theatrical culture.

It is observed that Tendulkar has not just contributed to the modern Marathi theatre but has given it a new dimension also. His plays disturb the audience by raising complex issues that remain unsettled even today in the contemporary society. It is the subtle and complex nature of his plays that gives him a place of pride in the international galaxy of playwrights. Originality in terms of intellectual approach and creativity in terms of imaginative sensibility are hallmarks of Tendulkar's dramatic genius. As a playwright with critical acumen, he is, at once, subjective and objective, personal and impersonal, particular and general, individual and social, and, finally, local and cosmopolitan.

In Tendulkar's plays, we have a glimpse of such great Western playwrights as Tennessee Williams, Arthur Miller, and Brecht. One can still feel a superb touch of Indianness in his plays. The folk form that is related only to the Marathi theatre such as *tamasha* and modes of recitation and story-telling specific to the region, some trends in the Sanskrit theatre such as *nandi* i.e., a play's beginning with a prayer to Lord Ganesha and *sutradhara* i.e., a character that plays a role akin to that of the chorus in Greek drama have been used effectively. Thus, Tendulkar's theatre may be said to have bridged the gulf between the traditional and the modern Indian theatre. The form *tamasha* has been used to expose the social and political evils, as, in *Ghashiram Kotwal*. The plays in general display their author's social concern and commitment. Instead of providing an escapist way through amusing scenes and situations, they are rather "engaged with the presentation of the problems of social inequality, the anguish and the disillusionment of the modern life, and the place of the individual in the society that is becoming hostile increasingly to the individual aspirations."[2]

Tendulkar is an individualist and, as such, presents an individual versus society. Thus, he stands for individual freedom. Having pinned his faith in the related values, he has been recognized as a pioneer of New Drama in Marathi. His plays put forth several questions without providing any answers to them. The playwright seeks to present the modern man with his predicament, his challenges, his difficulties, and his complexities. The life seen around is projected as it is and the dramatist makes no effort to moralize or philosophize it.

Most of Tendulkar's plays are seen as written in naturalistic vein. He depicts the scenes and situations from the day-to-day life. While portraying life as it is, his attention is, by and large, focused, not on the happy, gleeful aspects of life but on human weaknesses, follies, and foibles. He intends to make people conscious of their vices and limitations and, directly or indirectly, or even secretly wants them to mend their ways. In a limited sense, he may be seen as a silent social activist who covertly wishes to bring about a change in people's modes of thinking, feeling, and behaving. Despite all the pessimistic overtones of his plays, he is an optimist, and, as such, believes, maybe implicitly, that the world will be a better place to live in.

It is noticed that Tendulkar aims at giving the crude and banal aspects of life a dramatic garb. He uses drama as a means to raise questions rather than to provide solutions, but one cannot term his plays as problem plays like those of Ibsen, Shaw, or Galsworthy, since what the plays depict is the socio-cultural and political reality of human life. Tendulkar's plays do not give any message in explicit, clear-cut terms nor do they provide any clues or guidelines to the solutions of the problems they deal with. They are thought-provoking and evoke a note of silent protest in the minds of their audience.

The conservative people are stunned by the complex, problematic nature of Tendulkar's plays as he successfully tries to destroy outdated pieties and stereotyped beliefs. While dealing with the problems, reality is projected in all its vulgar and naked form. It is difficult to accept and appreciate the incident or event, but it is as real as inevitable. So, audience leaves the theatre with a disturbed mind. It is in this sense that Tendulkar can be seen as an iconoclast, who intends to bring about a silent, gradual change in people's attitude towards life and its problems.

The play *Silence! The Court is in Session* discusses the problem of unmarried motherhood through the conflict between an individual and society where innocence is ruthlessly crushed by cruelty; *The Vultures* exposes the evil tendencies inherent in human psyche that render people blind and transform them from human beings into loathsome animals; *Sakharam Binder* depicts excessive physical lust of a straightforward, angry, and frustrated man and destructive nature of a secretive woman; *Ghashiram Kotwal* dwells on the treacherous ways in power game; *Encounter in Umbugland,* focusing the political situation of India in 1971, represents Tendulkar's "New Woman" in the character of Vijaya who turns the tables on her treacherous male advisers; *Kamala* throws light on the evils in the so-called modern, cultured contemporary society and physical as well as mental exploitation of women within the family and outside it; *Kanyadan* may be seen as an indirect comment on the evil consequences of father's obsession with idealism and husband's obsession with caste consciousness. It is observed that the last three plays are topical in terms of thematic concerns and interests.

The function of art is not to provide answers or solutions but to raise questions. While exposing the foibles and hypocrisies of an individual *vis-à-vis* those of society, Tendulkar urges upon the audience to ponder over their problems. The play ends without offering any solutions to the audience who leave the theatre in a thinking, contemplative mood. The play's open-endedness may be seen as one of its striking features. In his article, "Vijay Tendulkar and the Metaphor of Violence," Sudhir Sonalkar rightly infers: In Tendulkar's plays, "...the ethical question remains both untouched and unanswered."[3] In the same vein, Asha S. Kanwar, too, observes:

> By leaving the ethical questions open, Tendulkar is perhaps inviting his audience to think about the solutions for themselves.[4]

In Tendulkar's plays, one can clearly see his acute observation of life. The events and incidents depicted in the plays have their origin in real life. A Tendulkar play can be seen as a mirror that reflects the individual's inner world and outer world. While projecting the social reality, he unveils two major tendencies of the Indian society: male dominance and feminine frailty. Women are projected as suffering a lot at the hands of their male-counterparts. They do not have equal status with men and, sometimes, part with their individual dignity, too. They are exploited both socially and economically. Although men are largely responsible for the exploitative and oppressive nature of society, women remain contributory to it. Here, the playwright seems to attack the Indian women's conservative minds, which do not allow them to show guts in encounter with their male-companions. Furthermore, they even provide them with an emotional support in a period of crisis. The tendency of enduring exploitation is so deep-rooted in their bones that even the thought of rebellion does not arise in their minds. They are hardly assertive and, at times, seem so slavish that their love and loyalty towards their husband and family do not allow them to raise any voice against them. Tendulkar's women characters, thus, appear to be the mute witnesses of the womankind's endless suffering in Indian society for centuries.

However, the character of Vijaya in *Encounter in Umbugland* is in sharp contrast with other female characters in Tendulkar's other plays. Her encounter with her ministers and her victory in it throw light on women's inherent power. Hostile circumstances play little, negligible role in shaping the good fortunes of such dominant people. The play's depiction of Vijaya's triumph over her rivals signals the inauguration of Women's Empowerment Decade (i.e. 2001 to 2010 A.D.).

Some of Tendulkar's plays are seen exploring the weaknesses of power politics. Outwardly, they appear historical; in reality, they are based on just particular historical incident or a current situation. Nevertheless, they are least topical and have a universal appeal. The ideas treated therein are relevant to all times and climes. The social situation depicted and the characters portrayed are beyond space and time. Such plays as *Encounter in Umbugland* and *Ghashiram Kotwal* deal with the theme of power and corruption. The former describes the victory of the individual against her rival group and the latter describes the defeat and dreadful end of the individual in conflict with society.

Another noteworthy quality of Tendulkar's plays is optimism. It characterizes his men and women who, despite the fact that they fall victims to the hostile circumstances, are stubbornly optimistic. Benare in *Silence! The Court is in Session* is cheated twice by her male-counterparts but she is happy with the thought that her body carries within it the witness of her love. Laxmi in *Sakharam Binder* remains happy thinking that she will die in solace with her head resting on Sakharam's lap. Rama in *The Vultures* endures suffering of the degraded or degenerate members of her family calmly and quietly in the hope that she will have her own child in future. Sarita in *Kamala* lives with her husband in the hope that she will have independent existence of her own in the years to come. The precarious situation in which all these four women are caught reveals the twin aspects of their character: (a) Indianness and (b) womanliness.

It is observed that in Tendulkar's plays most of the characters are the victims of chance or circumstance. Their actions are determined by the forces, which are out of their control. Psychologically speaking, heredity and environment play a major role in shaping their behaviour. The hostile circumstances in life leave some of them aggressive and violent, and others rather helpless and pitiable. Actually, most of them are animals disguised in human forms. They are to put it in Kumar Ketkar's words, "Tendulkar's Human Zoo."[5]

The protagonists of Tendulkar's plays such as Sakharam, Ghashiram, Jaisingh, Arun, etc., can be seen as anti-heroes, since each of them plays a major or central role in the play's action but lacks such qualities as dignity and courage that characterize a hero.

A remarkable feature of Tendulkar's plays is that they give us not an idealized but an actual portrayal of life with all its baser aspects that are an integral part of nature. However, audience can realize the dramatist's revolt against the established conventional norms and values and his ultimate demand or urge for a new code of conduct and morality. Thus, in the situations presented, Tendulkar, too, like Karl Marx, expects human beings to suffer as human beings, and not as animals. His characters are always seen standing with both feet firmly planted on the ground; never do they appear standing on "on stilts." So, his men and women, who inhabit the world of his plays, are made of the same clay as we ourselves are, they are very much like most of us with our flaws and failings, but aspire for happiness, peace, and freedom.

In the projection of life, Tendulkar appears to be a detached observer neither praising nor condemning either the cruel and violent characters or the kind and tender-hearted ones. A direct confrontation with banality, sordidness, and violence is difficult for audience to bear, as sometimes the characters appear more abominable and hateful than people in their actual lives.

One can easily observe that majority of the plays under discussion are related to the theme of love, sex, and violence. The angry and frustrated protagonists represent the post-1960 young generation in India. Bitter circumstances in life leave some of them rough and tough and others miserable and somewhat pitiable, too. But both the types of characters tend to win audience's sympathy. The playwright tries his best to remain a detached observer in the portrayal of characters but his silent compassion for the victims of chance or circumstance can be perceived.

The play *Silence! The Court is in Session* explores psychological violence of the frustrated people in the white-collar middle-class society; *The Vultures* depicts physical and verbal violence through the actions and the language of the characters; *Sakharam Binder* exhibits excessive physical lust of an angry man and helplessness of women, that compels them to bear physical and sexual violence of their master; *Ghashiram Kotwal* throws light on sadist tendencies of human nature and dreadful end of an innocent daughter and an over-ambitious father in power politics; *Kamala* exposes the hypocritical and selfish nature of the modern youths who use human beings as stepping-stones in achieving their goals; *Kanyadan* reveals a Dalit poet's psychological, physical, and verbal violence, which inheres in his ethos, familial background, and caste-consciousness.

In Tendulkar's plays, one can clearly perceive existential and absurd strains. The characters in his plays are themselves responsible for shaping their existence. His latest plays such as *Safar* (Cyclist) and *Niyatichya Bailala* (Damn, you Fate!) illustrate complexity and absurdity of present life. According to Chandrashekhar Barve, Tendulkar's plays "tend towards existentialism."[6] But such a contention cannot go uncontested, for the playwright is not given to any particular trend, nor does he take any avowedly philosophical stance, such as absurdity, or existentialism, or naturalism. In most of his plays, women play roles as prominent as men. He is not a downright feminist, however. There is, nevertheless, a fine blend of all these ideological inclinations and tendencies in his plays.

Tendulkar's writing, it is observed, is marked by a subtle satirical sense as his plays expose human follies and frailties. In his satire, there appears a harmonious combination of both the elements, i.e., Horatian and Juvenalian. Tendulkar's laughter is genial and his criticism is bitter. Thus, humour, wit, and irony are the hallmarks of his satirical talent. Apart from these, there are a few rhetorical speeches or poetic monologues and poems through which Tendulkar aims at revealing the psychological turmoil in the character's mind or objectifying the tense climactic situation, or the playwright's observations on life, e.g. Benare's final speech in *Silence!...* (116), Prannarayan's commentary and Pen-bearer's verses in *Encounter in Umbugland* (356 and 282, respectively), Rajaninath's poems in *The Vultures* (201-02) and Sutradhar and Others in *Ghashiram Kotwal* (617).

The function of Tendulkar's plays is neither to just entertain nor to just reveal ironies and contradictions but to help man know himself in relation to his environment. The plays depict agonies and sufferings, that is, in short, helplessness of man, but they are anti-sentimental and anti-emotional. They create cathartic feelings of pity and terror, since pathos and violence characterize most of the action in the plays. So, the total effect is neither of alienation nor of empathy but of creating necessary awareness in the audience. The chief impact of the play is one of shock, agitation, and awakening of the audience's mind and consciousness to the maladies and weaknesses of both, society and an individual. So, the playwright's aim is to transform drama from a means of entertainment into an object of enlightenment; in other words, he intends to make the theatre a medium of higher communication. To put it in Asha S. Kanwar's words:

> The effect produced by the play can be seen as neither one of 'empathy' as in the dramatic form of theatre nor one of 'alienation' as in the epic form of theatre but also akin to the Theatre of Cruelty so that the audience can understand the social process that leads to violence and cruelty, a malaise that Tendulkar has studied as a research project and effectively depicted in artistic form in his plays.[7]

The playwright's commitment to human values can be clearly perceived in his plays. The plays present a society divided on the basis of gender, class, caste, etc. Inequality, corruption, and violence characterize it. The life projected in the plays under study is miserable, full of contradictions, but it is real. Tendulkar's protagonists are sensitive, angry, and frustrated people, like most of us. This peculiar temperament of the protagonist disturbs the audience and gives them such a jerk that they are lulled out of their unconsciousness. It makes them introspective and, finally, sensitive to the issues of life. As a result, their outlook is broadened, their sensibility is sharpened, and their vision becomes clear.

What do Tendulkar's plays mean to the non-Indian readers or audience? What Erin B. Mee states in her Introduction to *Drama Contemporary* she has edited very well applies to the Tendulkar plays:

> I hope that each play will take people on a journey... however, the journey need not be to India: It can be a journey into one's self from a stance outside one's own cultural view-point.[8]

The study of Tendulkar's plays, to sum up, arrives at some significant inferences. The dramatist aims at bringing to light some of the most complex and vital issues of our existence, inner and outer. One can approach his plays from various points of view, such as psychological, sociological, politico-cultural, deterministic, existential, feminist, Marxist, etc. A brief, cursory but analytical treatment has been given here to all these aspects or dimensions of Tendulkar's plays. A modest, sincere attempt has been made in this work to present him as a man of the theatre with its variegated aspects.

Tendulkar's dramatic genius is characterized by unusual creativity, profound psychological insight, sharp, incisive sensibility, comprehensive vision and broad, cosmopolitan perspective. His plays are neither moral nor immoral. One may be justified in calling them amoral. Tendulkar is a moralist in the sense Shakespeare is a moralist—that is, in the highest sense of that word. One may critically examine his plays from dramaturgical point of view: As such, he can be seen as a master craftsman of dramatic art. See his situations, characterization, dialogues and the pauses therein and, finally, the tensions he builds up. All these, besides the stage directions, pose a challenge to the director.

The analytical study of Tendulkar's plays reveals that the dramatist has a desire to strive tirelessly for perfection of life where there are no barriers of caste, class, sex, etc., in society. He dreams, so to say, of freedom, equality, and social justice for one and all. Like Chekhov, he aims at creating a kind of emotionally refined, integrated, and conscious world. The playwright seems to share in Tagore's united, integrated sensibility in the lines quoted below from one of his songs in *Geetanjali.*

> Where the world has not been broken up into fragments by narrow domestic walls; Where tireless striving stretches its arms towards perfection; Where the clear stream of reason has not lost its way into the dreary desert sand of dead habit; Into that heaven of freedom, my Father, let my country awake.[9]

In the final analysis, Tendulkar's art may be seen as a liberating influence: It liberates us from our "cribbed, cabined, and confined" existence and helps us become, in one word, "human"—as human as possible.

NOTES

1. Arundhati Banerjee, Introduction, *Five Plays of Vijay Tendulkar,* Bombay: OUP, 1992, vii.
2. Asha S. Kanwar, *Ghashiram Kotwal: A Study Guide*, New Delhi: IGNOU, 1993, 12.
3. Sudhir Sonalkar, "Vijay Tendulkar and the Metaphor of Violence", *The Illustrated Weekly of India*, Nov. 20, 1983, 21. Quoted in Asha S. Kanwar, *Ghashiram Kotwal: A Study Guide,* New Delhi: IGNOU, 1993, 33.
4. Asha S. Kanwar, *Ghashiram Kotwal: A Study Guide*, New Delhi: IGNOU, 1993, 33.
5. Kumar Ketkar, "Tendulkar's Human Zoo", *The Illustrated Weekly*, Nov. 20, 1983, 22.
6. Chandrashekhar Barve, "The Man Who Explores the Depths of Life", (trans.) by Ajit Soman, Arun Belsare in Sudhakar Pandey and Freya Taraporwala (eds.), *Contemporary Indian Drama,* New Delhi: Prestige Books, 1990, 23.
7. Asha S. Kanwar, *Ghashiram Kotwal: A Study Guide*, New Delhi: IGNOU, 1993, 52.
8. Erin B. Mee (ed.), Introduction, *Drama Contemporary*, New Delhi: OUP, 2002, 18.
9. Rabindranath Tagore, *Geetanjali*, New Delhi: Macmillan.

TURNING POINT

2

Darwin's *Origin of the Species* (1859) is considered a milestone in the history of human evolution. It marks the beginning of the naturalistic movement in the different spheres of life. This movement never remains confined to science but has its impact on history, art, culture, criticism, and theatre. The contemporary life of people and their problems become the subject-matter of art and literature. Actual, real life situations that are mirrored in the plays make the theatre naturalistic. Such playwrights as Ibsen, Shaw, Sean O'Casey, T.S. Eliot, Tennessee Williams, Arthur Miller, etc., enrich the tradition of realistic plays with their innovative ideas and devices. Arthur Miller, Eugene O'Neill, and Tennessee Williams, the American playwrights, represent in their plays the inadequacies of modern man and the false values of the contemporary society. In the post-war period, T.S. Eliot, a poet, critic, and playwright deals with the psychological, religious, and secular problems of modern life in his poetic drama. Naturalistic elements go side by side with idealistic elements in the symbolic aspects of his poetic plays. In *Poetry and Drama,* the Harvard Lecture of 1950, he explains: "He wanted a poetic drama based on modern life, with people, living in apartments like us and using telephones and motor-cars."[1]

All these Euro-American playwrights use theatre not as a means of mere entertainment but as a means of bringing reformation in the thinking modes of people. They seek to make their audience introspective and encourage them to think of their day-to-day life problems allowing them to find out their own solutions.

For such plays of Shakespeare as *Measure for Measure, All's Well That Ends Well, Troilus and Cressida,* and *Hamlet,* E.M.W. Tillyard uses the term "problem plays."[2] According to Ernest Schanzer, "In Shakespeare's problem play, the moral issue, which is central to it, is presented in such a manner that we are unsure of our moral bearings, so that uncertain and divided responses to it in the minds of the audience are possible or even probable."[3]

Emile Zola, the French novelist, is convinced that only naturalistic movement can give vigour and life to the theatre, which will make it modern and new. The interest of Henrik Ibsen, the world-famous Norwegian dramatist, lies in using drama to ask questions rather than supply answers. He sees his own work, in Shaw's words, "as contribution to a forward struggle to give people new images of truth, images which at first they would inevitably be unable to accept."[4]

Ibsen's characters such as Nora, Barkman, etc., make the audience aware of the fact that freedom can be achieved or realized only by those who have the strength to see the world as it is. Nora's revolt against her husband takes her and all the audience away from the notion of home, sweet home. The womanly woman tries to face the bitter realities of actual world that is full of hardships and challenges. Her protest has a profound impact on the British playwrights as well as on the Indian playwrights, since she slams the door not only of her own home but of all homes that look sweet. The Natyamanwantar Theatre of the Marathi playwrights follow in the footsteps of Ibsen. Such major playwrights as Warerkar, Atre, Ranganekar, etc., are mainly concerned with the social problems of the day. In their plays, they consciously discuss the problems and bring out their varied aspects. Instead of presenting sentimental love scenes, they prefer to project on the stage truth to life, new morality, and social reality.

However, the theatre after 1956 marks a complete break with the previous theatre movement. Osborne's *Look Back in Anger* challenges the popularity of the problem plays of Ibsen, Shaw, Galsworthy, etc. The Indian playwrights such as Rakesh, Karnad, Tendulkar, and Sircar deal with the problems of the contemporary life. They represent life as it is, without trying to moralize or philosophize it in any way. The plays focus on man with all his complexities. However, the term "problem play" cannot be used for their plays like those of Shaw or Ibsen, since what they treat in their plays is not a social problem but an aspect of our socio-political and cultural life mostly on psychological level. Their plays such as *Silence! The Court is in Session, Nagamandala, Adhe Adhure, Procession,* etc., actually chart the course of avant-garde Indian theatre in the post-independence (to be more accurate, in the post-1960) period.

Vijay Tendulkar, originally a Marathi playwright, heralds a new school of drama like Harold Pinter and Edward Albee who handle new themes, new subjects, and new techniques. It is in this sense that Tendulkar modernizes the Marathi theatre. He uses the stage not to entertain the audience but to disturb them by shocking their sensibility, by making them aware of questions pertaining to human relationship and the reality of human existence.

The first play that sets him apart from the previous generation of the Marathi playwrights is *Manus Nawache Bet* (An Island Called Man). In it, he gives expression to the suffering of a solitary, modern individual in urban society. The plays that are instantly produced and performed such as *Madhlya Bhinti* (The Walls Between), *Chimniche Ghar Hote Menache* (The Nest of Wax), *Mee Jinklo, Mee Harlo* (I Won, I Lost), *Kavalyanchi Shala* (The School of Crows), and *Sari, Ga Sari* (Rain! O, Rain!) exhibit the beginning of avant-garde theatre in Marathi. A new wave begins in the Marathi theatre with the production of his *Silence! The Court is in Session, Sakharam Binder*, and *Ghashiram Kotwal*. The play *Silence! The Court is in Session* earns him a place among the leading Indian playwrights in the late sixties while *Ghashiram Kotwal* wins him an international fame in the mid-seventies and gives him a recognition as the vanguard not only of the Marathi theatre but of the Indian theatre also.

G.M. Kulkarni, a Marathi critic, observes:

> Like many other modern Marathi playwrights, Tendulkar follows the technique of Ibsen's plays in his early

> dramatic writing. However, the plays after 1963, reject this technique. Tendulkar succeeds in setting a "new form" by using the new, modern, folk, and classical elements simultaneously in his plays. This can be particularly noticed in his plays after the successful presentation of *Silence! The Court is in Session.*[5]

The play *Silence! The Court is in Session* is based on a real incident. The stimulus comes from an amateur group on its way to stage a mock trial in a village near Bombay. This play comes as a turning point in Tendulkar's career. It is a "play within a play" or a "play in the form of a rehearsal." In it, Tendulkar has raised several questions about love, sex, and moral values prevalent in society. To expose the hollowness of the middle class morality and dual standards of society, he makes ample use of irony, satire, pathos, and mock element. The success of the play lies in its universality. The questions raised by Benare, the central character of the play, exist in all ages and societies. Benare is projected as a rebel against the established values of the basically orthodox society. So, in a sense, she may be seen as Tendulkar's projection of a "New Woman" in the Indian context.

The action of the play revolves round the character of Leela Benare. She is presented as a female protagonist and her role eclipses the roles of her male-counterparts. In love, she is cheated twice; first by her maternal uncle and later by Prof. Damle, her loving-companion. However, in the first event, the guilt passes unnoticed and hence, unpunished. But, in the other one, she is caught in a trap, through the cruel game cunningly arranged by her companions, for her love affair has been already exposed by her pregnancy.

Each time Benare is disillusioned by her male-companions, for they love just her body and not her mind. Thinking of Prof. Damle as "an intellectual god" (118), she is sexually involved in a love affair with him. But he too, like her previous lover, is interested in her love just physically. Having fulfilled his sexual lust, he turns away, leaving her to suffer her fate in the so-called modern society.

Each time, Benare's counterparts successfully manoeuvre to victimize her, since she has no backing and support. She is forced to live a lonely, solitary life. So, it is easy for them to treat her as though she were a use-and-throw object. The tragedy of her life does not end with this only. Miss Benare becomes an object of ridicule among her companions who pose that they are the upholders of moral values of society. Benare is, therefore, made a scapegoat. She is ill treated by her colleagues. She suffers at their hands for the offence she has not committed. That is why she does not accept the punishment meted out to her: "infanticide" (actually, foeticide).

G.P. Deshpande, in his article entitled *Shantata! Court Chalu Ahe,* states:

> The play *Silence! The Court is in Session* is highly symbolic in nature. During the court proceedings of the mock-trial, such animals as dogs, a hen, etc., enter the hall. These animals symbolize an imbroglio of innocent, simple, and straightforward woman like Miss Benare (i.e., the hen) by cruel persons with dual personality (i.e., the dogs). So, the pursuit of the hen by the dogs symbolically represents Miss Benare's inhuman hunt by her fellow-companions.[6]

Violence that characterizes most of Tendulkar's plays makes its appearance felt in this play also. Through the torture of a helpless woman, Tendulkar throws light on the sadist tendencies of the middle-class people. All other characters except Samant fail to achieve the various aims they have in their respective lives. Mr. and Mrs. Kashikar remain childless, Ponkshe fails to be a scientist, Sukhatme to be a successful lawyer, Karnik to be an actor, and Rokde to gain an independent existence. In their attack on Benare, their hidden sense of failure surfaces and is clearly noticed. The dramatist indicates that the defeatism of the unsuccessful, frustrated men forces them to seek vicious pleasure in inflicting miseries on others, particularly those who are simple and innocent.

Benare's rhetorical soliloquy, at the end of the play, has become very famous in the contemporary Marathi theatre. But it is presented in such a way that it recreates a doubt in the mind of audience whether it is a soliloquy or self-defence suggesting, of course, in the final analysis that truth always gets suppressed in the proceedings of court, the fountain of justice! That is why Benare's objections seem to have been drowned by the judge's cry of silence and the banging of the gavel during the court proceedings. Her tragedy reveals that too much of innocence is unpardonable even in the so-called cultured society. Innocence is punished and cruelty is set free and, quite ironically, the play concludes with the words: "The show must go on" (120).

The play *The Vultures* is intensely morbid in the portrayal of its characters and action. It exposes greed, violence, selfishness, sensuality, and wickedness inherent in human nature through mutual interactions of the members of the family. All the family members except Rama and Rajaninath are leading a kind of life that is comparable to that of vultures only. They inherit the baser qualities from their father who cheats his own brother in business and acquires prosperity and affluence. Thus, the sons and the daughter follow in the footsteps of their father. They all belong to a flock of vultures.

Ramakant, Umakant, and Manik are, like their father, always ready to cheat one another and resort to extract more money. They do not hesitate to seek each other's lives to get a larger share of their father's property. Each one is suspicious of the other and loses the real treasure of life, that is, peace of mind. Manik's statement bears evidence to it. For she says to her sister-in-law Rama: "So, I should leave it (the door) open? Should I? So, you can come and strangle me, all of you? It's because I take care that I've survived in this house!" (207).

Ramakant and Umakant beat their father when he rejects to give them information about his secret account in a bank. When they could not get money from their sister's lover, the Raja of Hondur, they manoeuvre to abort her child in anguish by beating her inhumanly. Towards the end of the play, Manik successfully tries to abort the babe in the womb of her sister-in-law to avenge the wrong done to her by brothers. The actions of the characters i.e., the beating up of Hari Pitale by his sons, the forced abortions of Manik's and Rama's babes by Ramakant and Umakant and by Manik, respectively, the hatred that the family members have for each other "underline the fundamental evil inherent in human character."[7]

In Shakespeare's plays, the tragic hero is responsible for his death. So, we feel pity and sympathy for him. But in Tendulkar's play *The Vultures*, the characters are essentially bad without having a single good quality. Still, we feel sympathy for them rather than terror, as all these characters appear to be the victims of their own wickedness or viciousness. In their unceasing efforts to inflict miseries on others, they make their lives more miserable.

Another fact in the play that evokes criticism is Rama's illicit relationship with her half brother-in-law Rajaninath. Manik is blamed for having illicit love affair with the Raja of Hondur that results in her pregnancy. But Rama who is described as a sensitive, submissive, helpless, tender little bird among the vultures is shown sympathy despite the fact that, in love, she turns to Rajaninath and gets herself pregnant by him in the course of time. It is a positive achievement on the part of Tendulkar that he wins our sympathy for her right from the beginning of the play to its end. The reason for this is that Rama, having no other alternative, accepts the illicit relationship. Due to excessive, constant drinking, her husband grows impotent. Having no other source of happiness, she turns to Rajaninath, ignoring the social norms but following the dictates of her heart like Benare in *Silence! The Court is in Session,* and gets what she desires and deserves: That is motherhood, her natural, inherent right. However, she is helpless and cannot offer protection to the babe in her womb. Thus, like Benare, she too verges on becoming a tragic character.

In the play *Sakharam Binder,* Tendulkar, once again like in *The Vultures,* explores violence and sexual lust, deep-rooted in human nature, while projecting the complexity of human character. Each character in the play is the combination of strength and weakness, good and evil. Sakharam, the protagonist of the play, appears crude, aggressive, and violent. But, in his association with Laxmi, he displays tendencies of having been a religious and family loving man. As soon as Champa enters his life, all the desired changes evaporate, and he is shown as transformed into a sensual drunkard with perverted thoughts of sexual enjoyment. Laxmi, once the embodiment of an ideal Indian woman, tender, religious, and self-effacing, now turns out to be wicked and vicious when Champa becomes her rival in love. After Champa's murder, she shows greater presence of mind than Sakharam. Champa, who is apparently aggressive and violent like Sakharam, has a good deal of sympathy for Laxmi when the latter refuses to give her a shelter.

Sakharam, the book-binder, is an outcaste, having a Brahmin father and a Mahar mother. Due to the constant, inhuman beating of his father, he leaves his home at the age of eleven. The bitter experiences of life harden him and make him violent. In this sense, he may be said to inherit violence from his father. The frustrated household life in his childhood crushes his tender feeling and leaves him a rough and tough guy growing like a desert cactus that stands the onslaughts of stormy weather.

Having no belief in the institution of marriage, Sakharam remains a bachelor. But he makes a contractual arrangement based on mutual convenience with a woman in all her helplessness. Laxmi is the seventh in the series of such helpless women. She brings a noticeable change in his life but that relationship lasts for a short period. Her objection to join Daud, Sakharam's Muslim friend, in the prayer of Lord Ganapati annoys Sakharam and makes him violent. He beats her inhumanly. The result is that she leaves him instantly. Later, Champa enters Sakharam's life. All the good things end with her arrival, as he grows more violent, aggressive, and full of sexual passion. Still the playwright successfully manages to show intermittently goodness and sensitivity that are parts of his nature. His playing on *mridanga*, his rejection to Champa's touch on the morning of Dasara festival, for she does not have a bath, his feeling that Laxmi is far different from the previous women in his life—all these are the examples in the case. These aspects of his nature reveal that Sakharam is the victim not of his inherent weaknesses such as his viciousness, wickedness, etc., but of bitter circumstances in his life.

Marathi critics like D.V. Deshpande[8] and Tara Bhawalkar[9] describe Laxmi as sensitive, loyal, hard working and Champa as violent, aggressive, disloyal, etc. One finds it difficult to accept such a schism between Sakharam's women. Laxmi enters Sakharam's life, as her husband tortures her for she cannot bear a child from him. But the situation is not far different in her new home. She faces constant humiliation, severe beating, and excessive physical lust. Sakharam too, like her husband, refuses to give her a shelter on her return to him later. If she is willing to bear any amount of suffering with Sakharam, the question arises as to why she should not do so with her husband. She lives in Sakharam's house with a firm determination to die on his lap though she is ill treated and ill used by Champa. She claims for herself virtue and loyalty but finds nothing wrong about her relationship with an unknown man, Fouzdar Shinde. Laxmi confronts nothing less than a hell in Sakharam's house, she informs the latter of Champa's intimate association with Daud. In a way, she is responsible for Champa's murder. So, it is difficult to accept her as a generous and tender-hearted woman. Here, the playwright may be said to suggest that women themselves are responsible, at times, for their plight to a large extent. Vasant Palshikar describes the two women in contrast, thus:

> Laxmi's conversation with the insects and crows symbolically indicates her dissatisfaction with sexual passion. Her gleeful laughter, while she is speaking with the animals, incites Sakharam's sexual lust. Champa's physical beauty, her lovely appearance, inflame Sakharam's sexual hunger. Laxmi's behaviour, gestures, facial movements, and verbal expressions attract Sakharam towards her. Outwardly, she appears submissive, helpless, and docile but actually, she is ambitious, determined, possessive, and dictatorial.[10]

D.V. Deshpande and Tara Bhawalkar subject Champa to bitter criticism but it cannot be wholly justified for the reasons given below. Champa's violence is not without any reasons. Her mother shows utter disregard and carelessness for her. She sells her even before she grows mature. Later, again, the inhuman treatment she gets from her husband makes her coarse, violent, and aggressive. However, she shows sympathy to Laxmi and gives her shelter. Similarly, she rejects Sakharam to have an intercourse with her at the first night. She is touchy and sensitive to some of the issues of life. All these situations throw light on her real nature and bearing. The deterministic overtones of her life, like those of Sakharam's, are most perceptible and, hence, cannot be overlooked or brushed aside on the ground of morality.

Thus, in the play *Sakharam Binder,* Tendulkar presents life in all its ugliness and crudity. Such a naked reality, despite the fact that it is inevitable, is still difficult to believe. How to remove such rubbish from society is a question left for the audience to ponder over.

The play *Ghashiram Kotwal* is based on history but the chief focus is not on the historical situation, but on its relevance to the contemporary political scene. Tendulkar's plea printed on the blurb of the play goes thus:

> This is not a historical play. This is a non-historical opera-like legend based on a historical fact. Ghashiram is an offspring of a specific social situation. This social situation and this Ghashiram both go beyond time and place. Although the author undertakes all the responsibility of the historical base of the episode, he does not intend to express here his opinion on the Peshwa regime, Nana Phadnavis, and Ghashiram Kotwal in their so-called authentic life stories in the relevant history.[11]

Nevertheless, there are some Marathi critics, who downrightly condemn the play and criticize it, saying:

> If the playwright does not intend to express his opinion of the Peshwa regime, what else can be the intention of his writing the play? The question remains unanswered. The play's failure lies in its lack of intention.[12]

However, the play may be seen as a satire on the contemporary socio-political circumstances. Tendulkar depicts the circumstances in the Peshwa regime and thereby suggests that such circumstances are not confined to a particular era. They are seen in all times and climes.

Ghashiram is the protagonist of the play. He belongs not only to the late 18th century Peshwa regime but can be seen in any period of human history and in any corner of the globe. His rise and growth to power from Savaldas to the most controversial Kotwal of Poona is symbolic of the magnitude of corruption in our society. So, the incident in the play is historical but the way in which it is treated renders it universal. According to Girish Karnad, in *Ghashiram Kotwal,* Tendulkar uses "Dashavatara a traditional semi-classical form,"[13] and likens Ghashiram to the legendary giant Bhasmasura, who threatens to destroy his own creator.

Ghashiram goes to Poona to earn his livelihood. But he is tortured, humiliated, and banished from the city by the Brahmins. His cruelty springs up from his misery. He leaves Poona with a vow that he will return to Poona as well as seek revenge on the Brahmins by acquiring the position of Kotwal. To fulfil his vow, he uses his innocent, pretty daughter Gauri. Quite accidentally, Nana meets her in the temple of Lord Ganesha and is infatuated by her physical beauty and signals his desire to have sex with her. Ghashiram wants to make the most of the opportunity, and comes close to Nana, who offers him the position of Kotwal of the city. In return of this favour, he sends his innocent daughter to Nana. On becoming the Kotwal, Ghashiram moves recklessly. The city of Poona starts trembling at the mention of his name. The natural order for the time being stands wholly subverted: the destructive principle reigns supreme. It is a high water-mark; the tide turns and, in consequence, Gauri becomes a scapegoat of the power game. The report of Gauri's sudden death makes Ghashiram mad and ferocious. He repents his action, but has gone too far to return. So, he, too, thinks, like Macbeth, "Returning is as tedious as go over." "Once, he has sold his daughter to acquire power. Now, he accepts her death only to continue with the exercise of his power."[14] Nana, too, accepts the policy: "Use a thorn to take out a thorn" (63). Nana foresees that, in the days to come, Ghashiram will be extremely bitter with him. So, on his suggestion, the angry Brahmin mob surrounds Ghashiram and murders him, inflicting on him pitiless and inhuman troubles.

Thus, the play is a powerful satire on power politics. Through the story of Ghashiram, Tendulkar depicts the rise and growth in public life of the demons that are created by political leaders for the fulfilment of their selfish motives. Do-nothing fellows though they appear, they manage to achieve what they deserve. When these demons prove dangerous, they see to it and goad their confidants on to violently destroy them.

The play also explores the sad state of women in society. The idea projected is: Women have to subsist or survive at the whims and caprices of their male counterparts. The father Ghashiram does not hesitate in bargaining his daughter's chastity for the fulfilment of his political ambition. The situation, it seems, is not far different even in the present times.

The play is symbolic: It ends by suggesting some resultant ideas for discussion. The audience leaves the theatre with the consciousness that Ghashiram is dead only as a person while his role is very much alive. Somebody will play it. Ghashiram and Nana may be seen as ancestors of power-seekers irrespective of time and place. However, the playwright does not work out all the details. He just hints at the clue and leaves his audience to explore the ultimate truth of the situation and also of life at large.

The play *Encounter in Umbugland* is essentially a political allegory in the sense that the characters represent the historical personages and the story reveals the political situation in India of the late sixties and the early seventies. Soon after the death of Pandit Jawaharlal Nehru, the question arose "After Nehru, Who?" This question finds an echo in the play "After Vichitravirya, Who?" (284). In the portrayal of Prannarayan's character, "Tendulkar seems to draw heavily on his own observations of the world and the inhabitants around him."[15]

The play is steeped in political intrigues, designed to attain the position of authority. It is easy to identify the characters with the political figures that held ministerial positions in those years. More significant is the evolution of Princess Vijaya's character from a self-willed, whimsical, mischievous, and playful girl into an intelligent and ambitious dictator.

The play is a powerful satire on politics. It throws light on the fact that, in the political field, power is more important than duty. So, selfish designs have replaced selfless service. All the ideals behind the establishment of democracy—a state created by people for the welfare of people—remain just in its name. As soon as power changes, those at the top try to make the ruler collapse or reduce him to the stature of a pawn.

After the death of Vichitravirya, each minister tries his best to occupy the throne but none becomes successful in it due to the lack of unity. At last, they decide to make Vijaya their queen, the heiress of Vichitravirya. They have all devised a plan to rule the country in her name. Prannarayan teaches her how to be diplomatic in her relations with others. At first, Vijaya rejects all this as she wishes to enjoy her freedom. But in the course of time, she learns enjoying power, and, power-drunk, she succeeds in suppressing her humanity. Towards the end of the play, she comes out victorious over her rivals.

The role of Prannarayan is very significant. His function in the play is the same as that of a *sutradhara* or a chorus. As such, he is presented as a detached observer and neutral, patient commentator. It is through his comments that the audience becomes aware of the ugliness and futility of the power game and it is through his eyes that the playwright brings forth the central concern of the play: "Power corrupts itself; absolute power corrupts absolutely."

With the publication of this play, it becomes quite evident that, in the field of power politics, nothing is real: appearances are deceptive; success and treachery go hand in hand. "One should take stock of the situation—give some advantages, and get some. Politics means sweetly smiling enmity and the experience of sacrifice. A show of sacrifice is always profitable in politics" (306). A ruler should always remind that each of the persons is more important than the next. The self-importance of the subjects should not suffer at any rate. Actually, all those things are difficult to accept for a man of truth. So, the ruler has not to be human, but superhuman or even divine. One should not be true to oneself in politics. Princess Vijaya's development from a headstrong, inexperienced princess to a prudent, intelligent ruler provides a proof to the fact that a ruler learns all those tricks of the trade gradually in the course of time. The playwright makes his readers conscious of the ugliness, corruption, and treachery in politics and stimulates them to think over them.

Within its limits, the play comprises a satire on journalism also. The technique of the two masked men, bearing out-sized pens and mouthing with remarks, is used at regular intervals. They provide information about the political feuds so that apparently objective observation may be made. Actually, these two masked men fulfil the objective of the newspaper. In her critical introduction to the book, Arundhati Banerjee states:

> In their observation, one can hear an echo of the cynical tone of the headlines, published daily in our newspapers—ultimately meaningless statements that resolve nothing but aggravate existing problems.[16]

The play *Kamala* is based on a real-life incident. Ashwin Sarin, the then correspondent editor of *The Indian Express* fetched a girl from a rural flesh-market and presented her at the press conference. Representing this real incident, Tendulkar throws light on the ghastly flesh market, the position of women in society, the cut-throat competition that goes on in the success-oriented contemporary generation, and the egoistic hypocrisy of the young journalists.

Likewise, in the play, a young journalist Jaisingh Jadhav brings a girl named Kamala from a rural flesh market and presents her at the press conference. He accepts such a dangerous task not with a view to reforming Kamala's life but as a part of his professional commitment. Kamala, for him, is a means by which he can get a promotion in his job and win reputation in his professional career. "He never stops to think what will happen to Kamala after this expose."[17] Craze for both money and success renders him loveless as well as mindless.

The concept of newspaper reporting is shown in some critical light. The real-life incident in the play highlights the unbearable fact that a newspaper, the so-called means of social reform, is transformed into an object of getting name, position, and money. Jaisingh represents the success-oriented, sophisticated individual who is willing to sacrifice human values in the pursuit of his goals. Helpless people like Kamala cannot help becoming scapegoats then.

The play also consists of a critique on Indian family system, where women are used either as slaves, menial servants, or stepping stones by their male counterparts. However, they themselves are responsible for their plight. Sarita becomes conscious of the selfish hypocrisy of her husband and of the fact that her position in the house is not far different from Kamala's. But she lacks the spirit to rebel against her husband. Instead, she provides him an emotional support, when he is fired.

The play *Kanyadan* is perhaps the most controversial of Tendulkar's plays. It deals with psychological study of the social tensions caused by casteism in India side by side with the development of Jyoti's character from a soft-spoken and highly cultured Brahmin girl into a hardened spouse of her dalit husband. Likewise, it portrays transformation in Nath's attitude. Bitter experiences of life turn the stubborn idealist into a disillusioned realist.

Nath is an MLA and Seva, his wife, is a social activist. They cannot spare sufficient time for the upbringing of their children Jyoti and Jaiprakash. Nath always stays outside the house doing social service and delivering public speeches. Seva is often busy organizing women's rallies and camps. Here, the playwright throws light on the fact that, in the contemporary society, educated parents become oblivious of their familial responsibility of tending their children while fulfilling their social obligations.

The play, as the title suggests, centres round the theme of matrimonial relationship. Jyoti, an educated lady, hails from a politically and socially conscious Brahmin family. She decides to marry Arun Athawale, a young Dalit poet. Her brother and mother forewarn her about the misery that may befall her in the aftermath of the marriage. However, her idealist father, who dreams of a casteless society, appreciates her decision since he believes that society cannot be transformed through words alone. Jyoti's decision to marry Arun provides him an opportunity to follow in the footsteps of the old social reformers who not only delivered speeches and wrote articles on the remarriages of widows but also married them. So, Jyoti and Arun get married. "What follows is a sequence of violence, misery, and disllusionment."[18]

Arun always remains conscious of his lower class origin and inflicts on Jyoti inhumane cruelties. Constant awareness of the suffering which the Dalits have undergone such as eating stale, stinking bread, flesh of dead animals, etc., renders him violent. He is of the opinion that there cannot be any give-and-take between the Dalits and upper-class people. The constant memory of the incident that even the call of the downtrodden, "Johaar, Maayi-Baap! Sir/Madam, Sweeper!" (513) pollutes the Brahmins' ears makes him restless and mindless. He comes to the conclusion that the Dalits cannot fit into the Brahmins' "unwrinkled Tinopal world" (513). So, the hellish sufferings that Jyoti receives in her matrimonial life with Arun is a kind of revenge that he seeks on the Brahmins for having humiliated and exploited his ancestors for centuries.

All the efforts of her mother and brother to rescue Jyoti from the horrible suffering come to noting. Her father compels her to go with Arun, as he is not ready to give up his ideals. It is so because, he believes: "No man is fundamentally evil; he is good. He has certain propensities towards evil. They must be transformed, completely uprooted and destroyed. And then, the earth will become heaven. It is essential to awaken the good slumbering within man..." (563).

Nath always dreams of freedom, equality, and social justice for one and all. For him, his daughter's marriage with a Dalit boy is a kind of successful gesture towards his efforts of creating an egalitarian, humanitarian society where human beings are treated as human beings and not as animals. Rational in thinking as his wife and son are, they refuse to share his united, integrated sensibility. This is how he urges upon his wife to save the intercaste marriage; he pleads (with passion): "Seva, let not this wonderful experiment fail. This dream, which is struggling to turn real, let it not crumble into dust before our eyes! We have to do something. We must save this marriage" (537).

However, in the course of time, Nath realizes the hollowness of his idealism. Arun receives a high acclaim for his autobiography. Name, fame, and position in society do not bring about any change in the brutal treatment he metes out to his wife. He beats and kicks Jyoti even during her pregnancy. The physical torture becomes a routine affair with her. But she cannot bear him insulting her parents by calling her mother a "procuress" who supplies girls from the Seva-dal to the socialist leaders, and again, her father a 'eunuch.' It is difficult for Nath to believe the fact that the person who describes the humiliations he has experienced with extraordinary sensitivity and seeks sadistic pleasure in wreaking revenge upon his wife for the guilts of her class or earlier generations. Father feels guilt-conscious thinking that his daughter becomes painful and miserable for having sincerely adopted his scale of values on the path of humanism.

Nath fails to comprehend Arun's split personality. Somehow or the other, he wants to help him, but finds himself too helpless to do anything. On the contrary, he goes to deliver a speech on his autobiography thinking that his refusal to speak on it will invite more troubles for Jyoti. But she does not like her father's appeasing policy in making an insincere, dishonest speech. She accuses him of having made her mentally crippled and abandons his house with a firm decision never to return.

Returning is not possible for Jyoti. Her father has taught her all through her life that it is cowardly to bow down to circumstances. She is reminded of the lines from one of Kusumagraja's poems which her father often recites "I march with utter faith in the goal; I grow with rising hopes, cowards stay ashore, every wave opens a path for me" (565). The lines act like a drug on her consciousness, so intensely and poignantly, that it becomes impossible for her to abandon the path (of an intercaste marriage) she has treaded so far. The play is open-ended and, hence, the audience is left to ponder over what happens to the daughter's prospects of married life and the father's idealistic fervour in the days to come.

The play *A Friend's Story* deals with a bold theme of lesbianism. The action of the play moves round the central character of Sumitra Dev, i.e., Mitra. The playwright develops the character of Mitra through the comments of Bapu whose role is similar to that of sutradhara in Sanskrit plays or that of chorus in Greek plays.

The subject of the play is different as well as daring. Mitra is portrayed as having physical hormonal imbalance. She herself is conscious of the fact that she is distinct from other girls having a stubborn nature like that of a boy—always following her instincts. She is reckless in the sense of being quite careless of social norms and moral values.

The play begins with Bapu talking to himself. He is in the first year degree class. Sumitra comes from somewhere and joins the college as the second year B.A. student. While introducing her character Bapu says: "...there was a masculine vigour in Sumitra Dev's stride and speech. She was carefree, her laughter came in loud bursts. She had eyes which met you in straight combat. Her broad forehead suggested intelligence. Her entire personality had a natural, aggressive masculinity, but with a figure irresistibly attractive to men" (419).

Bapu comes across Mitra's photograph on the floor in the college's corridor smoking cigarette with two hairy, bare-chested men. Observing it, he is taken aback. But he notices that Mitra remains quite normal while accepting it from him. She offers him a cup of tea and also a proposal for friendship.

Mitra has masculine traits in her character right from her childhood. She always likes to play with boys and also their games. She never feels shy or embarrassed if the boys handles her roughly as they play together. The elders in the family get worried and fix her marriage with a decent boy. They intentionally create opportunities for the two to meet in privacy.

Although Mitra tries her best, she fails to develop man-woman relationship. In the close intimacy with men, she feels no physical thrill, no excitement. She becomes restless with the thought as to how and why she feels comfortable (instead of feeling shy) in the company of men. She realizes that she likes the company of men, but cannot appreciate their ways with women. So, she tries to commit suicide but is frustrated in the attempt. After this incident, she decides to accept life as it is and

> ...then allows herself to flow with the stream, and lets herself go. The reasons for this are, her stubborn nature, her desire to do what she wants to do, social conflict, and then...her rebellion. There is one person who tries to understand her and that is Bapu...(who) always helps her....[19]

Bapu likes Mitra and he accepts her as a friend with all her deficiencies. It seems that the relationship between Bapu and Mitra remains unique due to him alone. The audience studies and understands Mitra's character in the light of his remarks. Throughout the play, it is only he who supports her. Very frankly, she confesses to Bapu the fact of her being abnormal. He tries to understand her and sympathise with her.

Mitra seems to be the one who caters to her own physical needs irrespective of what others may think of her behaviour. She is straightforward and frank in her friendship with Bapu. It is just her second meeting when, she clutches his hand and presses it hard, rather savagely and then asks him: "What did you feel when I held your hand?... How did my hand feel to you?... Come on, tell me" (425). Without any reservation, she discloses to him the secret that she cannot play the role of a fiancée or a wife.

It is not only Mitra's thinking that indicates that she is abnormal, but her gestures, features, mannerisms also suggest it. While narrating her physical problem, she is aware that she is hardly sentsitive to the oppsite sex's appeal. Like a man, she takes out a cigarette and lights it. Her hand trembles and she holds Bapu for support. He notices a turbulent storm raking within her. Tranquillity returns and she stubs out the cigarette and flings it away. Mitra has full confidence in her friend who is well aware of the fact that her outward appearance is rather deceptive. Behind her loud, full-throated, masculine laughter and her repeated statement, "I don't care", is hidden a great deal of restlessness.

The second and the third acts deal with Mitra's relationship with Nama, Pande's attraction towards Mitra, Manya Dalvi's revolt against Mitra, and her ultimate pathetic end.

Pande, the secretary of drama in college makes an offer to Mitra to play a male role to which she responds positively. Nama, a delicate, doll-like girl plays the heroine. In the actual performance of the play, particularly, in the love-scene, Mitra looks commanding in her male role. The whistles, comments, and claps from students have no impact on her. After the performance, while Nama is about to leave, Mitra strides up to her, hugs her tight, and kisses her, saying "Good night, darling, and sweet dreams" (436). She is sexually drawn towards Nama. She openly makes a revelation to Bapu about her experience. "I lost control. Her touch.... Her very desirable body in my arms...she moved away as if she sensed it" (440).

As Mitra likes Nama, Pande likes Mitra. However, he cannot convey his feelings. Without Mitra, he finds life meaningless. In desperateness, he joins army and goes straight to the battle front.

Bapu helps Mitra in her relationship with Nama although he is threatened and beaten by the latter's boy-friend Dalvi. Bapu's room is used as a meeting place. Nama, in the beginning, enjoys Mitra's company but very soon gets bored, since she goes to the extreme in her gesture or exercise. So, she finds it difficult to cope with her. That is why she concedes: "She loves me... very much. I too like the way she treats me.... But sometimes I get fed up even with her love..." (469). Bapu tries his best to convince Mitra of the fact that hers is an obsolutely wrong path; it is rather bad. So, it will be better to give up the relationship and forget Nama. However, his suggestion goes futile since Mitra pays no heed to it.

Nama's character is a complex one. As a result, her involvement with Mitra seems quite confusing. She represents the class of the girls who enjoys love relationship but lacks the courage to face the ultimate consequences. She neither remains loyal to her relationship with Mitra nor accepts Dalvi as her life partner. Instead, she prefers to go to Calcutta and get married to a stranger. So, like Jyoti, in the play *Kanyadan*, Nama, too, appears, to use Ramesh Dhongade's words, "...rather hollow, loose, and lacking backbone."[20]

Considering Mitra as his rival in his love-affair with Nama, Dalvi resolves to ruin her. He successfully tries to expose her deficiency through letters. As a result, Mitra is rusticated from college. Her family members refuse to give her any support. In her article titled "Note on *A Friend's Story*," Rohini Hattangady says:

> ...Bapu is the main support for her when Bapu, too, doesn't understand her...she is angry at Bapu and at herself, and breaks away from him. For Mitra, it is not breaking away from Bapu but breaking away from herself, from her being Mitra. She tries to be 'feminine' (but in vain)...and one day commits suicide—and succeeds![21]

Mitra becomes miserable due to her physical deformity. In the later part of the play, it becomes an open secret. But nobody takes any cognizance of it. Even her family members remain indifferent. Instead of consulting a doctor or a psychiatrist, they leave her to suffer her lot. Whether there is or is not any remedy for this deformity is a million dollar question left for the audience to ponder over.

To make the matter worse, the other two characters Nama and Manya Dalvi also seem to suffer from mental deformity. Nama remains faithful neither to Mitra nor to Dalvi. That she is interested in neither of them is perceived from the very beginning. She just enjoys their company. She willingly meets Mitra in Bapu's room. But when Dalvi visits the room accidentally, he asks her indignantly to leave and she follows him without caring for Mitra's feelings. Mitra gets angry, not because she is insulted by Dalvi's abusive words but because Nama follows him straightway. Towards the end of the play, a slight hint is given that Dalvi has an affair with a new girl; everything is over between Dalvi-Nama relationship. Still he firmly determines to ruin Mitra. He is one of those who derive vicious pleasure in inflicting miseries on others.

At the beginning of the play, Bapu introduces himself as: "No professor could have recalled my name without some effort. I was one of the crowd who entered college solely for filling the benches in the classroom" (420). Here, the playwright seems to throw light on the inferiority complex that exists in majority of the youths who fail to bring out the best within them. Even education cannot be seen as a liberating force for them. The play is open-ended. The audience are left to find out their own remedies for the problem that remains burning in all times and climes.

The whole discussion above leads one to say what Emile Zola states about naturalism, very well apts to Tendulkar's plays:

> It is necessary to accept nature as she is, without modifying her. The Work becomes an official record, nothing more; its only merit is that of exact observation of life as it is.[22]

Tendulkar does not believe in the dictum "Art for Art's Sake." Instead, he believes, unlike the advocates of aestheticism, in art as propaganda. Nevertheless, he cannot be called a sheer propagandist. That is why, in his plays, life is presented as it is with all its vices, drawbacks, and weaknesses. His plays refuse to offer strained coherence or show a path of revelation. He strictly follows what Chekhov does and states: "Life on the stage should be as it really is, and the people, too, should be as they are and not on stilts."[23]

For Ibsen and Shaw, the success and the worthiness of a play depend upon the fact to what extent it effects the transformation of man. Their main objective is to bring about a revolutionary change in an individual's mind. They are convinced that it could not be carried out in the existing theatre but in "a new house of drama," supported by "the pillars of truth and freedom."[24]

Tendulkar, in his plays, successfully tries to give the socio-political and cultural reality of his age a dramatic garb. Theatre is his chosen medium, through which he visualizes and addresses himself to the task of developing a really cultured human personality. Everything he produces and performs on the stage has its origin in real life. He presents a situation in which the protagonist's mind catches light or develops insight compelling the audience to accept life as it is and with all its challenges.

Tendulkar, in his plays, successfully tries to destroy the outdated pieties and stereotyped beliefs. He is an iconoclast who intends to bring about a change not only in the subject-matter, form, and structure of his plays but also in the mind-set of his audience. In a Tendulkar play, to say it in Eric Bentley's words, "We move beyond a character's personality to his humanity."[25] Leela Benare, like Nora, is one of the New Women who enables us to face the bitter realities of actual life. However, freedom is achieved at last by sacrificing pleasure.

Tendulkar's plays, in general, throw a flood of light on the complexity of human relationship. The connected themes of his plays under discussion are concerned, in one way or another, with love, sex, and violence. However, the content or the subject-matter of each of the plays is distinct from and independent of the other.

The play *Silence! The Court is in Session* depicts the conflict of innocence versus cruelty through the tragedy of a simple, innocent, and straightforward teacher victimized by the society; *The Vultures* represents a degenerate family where there is an utter defeat of humanity against monstrosity; *Sakharam Binder* explores the complexity of human nature where the characters simultaneously represent a strange combination of sensibility and insensibility; *Kamala* exhibits the corrupt, success-oriented, modern society in which simple, innocent, and sensitive people like Kamala and Sarita become scapegoats of the treacherous ways of the so-called cultured, civilized and progressive people; *Ghashiram Kotwal* is a satire on power politics, in which deterministic overtones of human life are most perceptible through the life-story of Ghashiram; and *Kanyadan* deals with the theme of conflict between idealism versus reality. The play *Encounter in Umbugland* differs from other plays in that the problematic aspects presented here are related to the dangerous game played in power politics. Treacherous ways are devised and adopted to gain the position of authority as to help Princess Vijaya triumph over her ministers by suppressing her humanity. Through her character, Tendulkar seems to state the idea that the people who believe in the truth of the axiomatic statement —"My mind is my master and my thoughts are my power."— always remain victorious.

The generation portrayed is a culturally, ethically, and mentally crippled one. People suffer from incomprehension and fall victims to wilful monstrosity. The playwright takes liberty of using harsh, incisive, and at times rough language to represent negative (animal) and positive (human) aspects of the "lost" or doomed generation.

Thus, Tendulkar uses the stage not as a means to provide entertainment but to bring about a change or reformation in the attitude of people. He prevents the emotional involvement of the audience and enables them, with more or less unconcernedly to judge the play as detached observers. His plays seem to move closer to the established norms or traditions of the Euro-American 20th Century Drama. In his early days, he has been greatly influenced by Western films and playwrights. He uses their techniques successfully in his plays e.g., Shakespeare's technique of 'play within the play', his dramatic device of "mask" as reflected in the "two masked men" in the play *Encounter in Umbugland,* Pirandello's "Intimate Theatre" in the play *Silence! The Court is in Session*, the concept of a "New Woman" in such characters as Miss Benare, Vijaya, Sarita, etc. However, he gives them a superb touch of Indianness by using indigenous techniques in a highly original and individualized way. His contribution to the Contemporary Indian Theatre is unique in this respect and, hence, remains without a parallel. Ulhas Luktuke is quite justified in pointing out:

> Tendulkar's plays broaden the ambit of the Marathi plays. He gives expression to the banality of every day life of common people in a dramatic form. After the successful presentation of *Silence! The Court is in Session*, he brings psychological realism in his plays

through the discussion of various problems. He has fathered a new world of sensibility. That is his greatest contribution to Marathi Literature and Theatre.[26]

NOTES

1. T.S. Eliot, "The Family Reunion", Ronald Gaskell (ed.), *Drama and Reality,* London: Routledge and Kegan Paul, 1972, 129.
2. E.M.W. Tillyard, Introduction, *Shakespeare's Problem Plays,* London: Chatto and Windus, 1950, I.
3. Earnest Schanzer, *The Problem Plays of Shakespeare,* London: Routledge and Kegan Paul, 1963, 8.
4. Nicholas Grene, *Bernard Shaw: A Critical View,* London: Macmillan, 1984, 7.
5. G.M. Kulkarni, "Natakkar Vijay Tendulkar, Ek Jinkane, Harne", *Satyakatha,* Dec., 1971, 38, translated by the Investigator herself.
6. G.P. Deshpande, "Shantata! Court Chalu Ahe: Kahi Vichar", *Satyakatha,* 1972, 23. The extract is a translation in English by the Investigator herself.
7. Arundhati Banerjee, Introduction, *Five Plays of Vijay Tendulkar,* Bombay: OUP, 1992, XII.
8. D.V. Deshpande, *Mala Disaleli Natake,* Pune: Raviraj Publication, 1989, 9.
9. Tara Bhawalkar, *Marathi Natak: Nawya Disha, Nawi Walne,* Pune: Mehta Publication, 1997, 68 and 72.
10. Vasant Palshikar, "Sakharam Binder", *Pratishthan,* May, 1973, 13-14. Translated by the investigator herself.
11. Vijay Tendulkar, *Ghashiram Kotwal,* Pune: Nilkanth Publication, IV edition, 1992, translated into English by the investigator herself.
12. "*Ghashiram Kotwal:* Vijay Tendulkar", *Alochana,* Pune: Nilkanth Publication, May, 1973, 27. The Marathi critical remarks are rendered in translation by the present investigator.
13. Girish Karnad, Introduction, *Three Plays,* New Delhi: OUP, 1994, 15. Quoted in Manchi Sarat Babu, *Indian Drama Today,* New Delhi: Prestige Books, 1997, 72.
14. Manchi Sarat Babu, *Indian Drama Today,* New Delhi: Prestige Books, 1997, 76.
15. N.S. Dharan, *The Plays of Vijay Tendulkar,* New Delhi: Creative Books, 1999, 86.
16. Arundhati Banerjee, Introduction, *Five Plays of Vijay Tendulkar,* Bombay: OUP, 1992, XI.
17. *Ibid.*, xvii.
18. N.S. Dharan, *The Plays of Vijay Tendulkar*, New Delhi: Creative Books, 1999, 88.

19. Rohini Hattangady, Appendix III, "Note on *A Friend's Story*", *Collected Plays in Translation*, New Delhi: OUP, 2003, 594.
20. Ramesh Dhongade, "*Kanyadan*, Apayashanchya Maliketil Ek Bhar", *Natyadarpan*, Oct., 1983, 5. The Marathi critical remark is a translation by the investigator herself.
21. Rohini Hattangady, Appendix III, "Note on *A Friend's Story*", *Collected Plays in Translation*, New Delhi: OUP, 2003, 595.
22. John Lahr, "Pinter and Chekhov: The Bond of Naturalism", in Arthur Ganz (Ed.), *Pinter: A Collection of Critical Essays* (A spectrum book 20th Century Views), London: Prentice-Hall International, 1972, 60.
23. David Magarshack, *Chekhov, The Dramatist,* New York: Hill and Wang, 1960, 84.
24. J.D. Dhingra, *Ibsen and Shaw: A Critical Evaluation,* Vol. 1, Jalandhar: ABS Publication, 1991, 38.
25. Ronald Gaskell, *Drama and Reality,* London: Routledge and Kegan Paul, 1972, 95.
26. Ulhas Luktuke, "Abhar! Rangachya Ewadhya Tukadyasathi", *Kesari,* Mar. 29, 1970, 9. Translated by the investigator herself.

CANDID SCRUTINY

3

The development of the problem plays towards the close of the Victorian age marks the rise and growth of the naturalistic movement in the European theatre which brings innovations in themes and structure of the plays. Such playwrights as Ibsen, Shaw, etc., have adopted the mode of naturalistic drama. The actual contemporary life becomes the subject-matter of their plays. The playwrights depict and discuss the problems of the day-to-day life of people thoroughly but do not suggest any solution to the problems. So, the audience becomes the active participant in the appreciation of the plays. However, the popularity of the English problem plays is later challenged by the poetic and experimental plays of the post-war new drama, particularly by Osborne's presentation of his play *Look Back in Anger* on May 8, 1956.

Such a break is conspicuously noticed in the post-independence Indian theatre, since the Marathi playwright Tendulkar consciously or unconsciously plays sedulous ape to the new trends in the post-war Anglo-American drama. His plays depict the problematic nature of contemporary Indian social life. They project anger, violence, and frustration of the post-independence young generation in India.

However, the plays are not merely topical. Using the real-life incidents, Tendulkar raises certain issues that are faced by all societies in all times and climes.

> Topicality and timelessness combine to create an enigma around Vijay Tendulkar's plays.... The fierce controversy surrounding his plays...is perhaps an obvious

> indicator of their currency, their strong rootedness in the socio-political context in which they were written. At the same time, the magnetic quality of the plays, reflected in the frequency with which they continue to be performed in different parts of India and abroad, suggests a certain universal quality.[1]

It is observed that Tendulkar's plays reflect socio-cultural reality as they comprise real-life situations, events, and incidents. The playwright himself has either witnessed or heard of most of the major characters at one point of time or the other of his life.

While reflecting socio-political reality, man is exhibited totally helpless against the bitter circumstances in life in the modern world. The playwright's sympathy for the "little big man"[2] in the modern world and for the women who are victims of social and familial norms and values is clearly perceptible.

The plays, directly or indirectly, bring to notice man's response to ordinary, day-to-day life and his total helplessness against the forces of fate, that is, the role played by chance or circumstance in his life. No doubt, that most of the characters are aggressive, violent, and sensual, but circumstances play a major role in shaping their respective lives, natures, and personalities. The sensitive, tender-hearted and generous characters become miserable and lead their lives as victims of circumstances.

> Today in every modern Indian language, one can discern many schools of theatre—the "traditional", the experimental, and the post-modernist. Tendulkar is a traditional artist with extraordinary talents, and his plays reveal modernist qualities. He received the attention of artists during the seventies and in his plays are found two dominant modes, irony and satire, which, of course, were written elaborately in ancient India.[3]

Tendulkar is one of the earliest Indian playwrights to advocate the new social drama. In his plays such as *Silence! The Court is in Session, Encounter in Umbugland, The Vultures,* etc., he deals with the problems such as marriage, sex, power politics, violence, etc. He diagnoses the ills and evils of contemporary society with a view to bringing reformation in the mind-set of people. Most of his plays deal with the white-collar, middle-class society, its problems, and the protagonist's effort is, obliquely or implicitly, directed towards solving these problems.

Tendulkar is not a "traditional" (as contended by R. Balchandran in the quotation above) but a new playwright. He marks a definite break with the mainstream Marathi drama as well as Indian drama as he represents life with all its multifold aspects such as ugliness, crudity, vulgarity, etc.

The essential characteristic of Tendulkar's plays is that they present a perplexing, distressing, and complex situation in all seriousness. They carry no message, in overt or covert terms. He minces no words in moralizing or philosophizing. He presents the existing reality of human predicament, as he perceives it with his own naked eyes. With the treatment of the details of actual life, his plays become more and more realistic. Besides, the ideas put forward in the plays are thought-provoking and revolutionary. Tendulkar opines:

> I think a lot before I write. My creativity has been shaped more by experience than by imagination.[4]

In an interview with K. Kannan, he identifies writing with life, and life with writing and states: "If I stop writing some day, life itself will stop for me."[5]

Most of his plays are based on real-life incidents. The play *Kanyadan* is supposed to depict the life of a Dalit poet Namdeo Dhasal; *Silence! The Court is in Session* is modelled on actual dialogues the dramatist has heard at a mock-trial enacted by a group of players; *Ghashiram Kotwal* is constructed on the basis of a historical incident in the Peshwa regime; *Kamala* has its genesis in the actual happenings appeared in the newspaper. The play *A Friend's Story* is based on the life story of a person whom Tendulkar comes across in Pune.

Tendulkar's plays manifest his strong dissatisfaction with the prevailing social order. They deal with miseries and sufferings caused by the cruel forces and conventions of society. The world he has projected looks strange or fantastic at times, but it is real. All his articles, stories, and plays reveal that the tone of his writing is realistic, at times satirical and poignant. Arundhati Banerjee points out:

> Tendulkar presents modern man in all his complexities. He portrays life as it is from different angles, without trying to moralize or philosophize in any way. All the works contain a latent critique of modern Indian society, mostly middle-class and lower middle-class, though from different angles.[6]

Tendulkar is an avant-garde playwright for he deliberately undertakes, in Ezra Pound's phrase 'to make it new.'[7] He had shocked the sensibility of the conventional, traditional readers by revolting against the accepted norms and values and by introducing the neglected, and sometimes the forbidden, subject-matter. He has handled the subject-matters in such a way that the audience becomes conscious of the fact that sometimes the great thoughts of eminent personalities appear rather hallow. Mrs. Indira Gandhi says:

> Education is a liberating force and, in our age, it is also a democratizing force, cutting across the barriers of caste and class, smoothing out the inequalities imposed upon us by birth and other circumstances.[8]

By and large, the statement is true, but sounds contradictory in the light of Tendulkar's plays *Silence! The Court is in Session* and *Kamala.* The central female characters in these plays Benare and Sarita represent the modern, educated, sophisticated ladies of society. But mere formal education has not solved their problems. It is observed education has not enabled us to overcome the traditional barriers of sex-discrimination, and women still fall victims to the male-dominated society.

> Tendulkar's plays are notable for their uncompromising realism, merciless probing of human nature, candid scrutiny of individual and group psychology, and experimental technique.[9]

They relentlessly and ruthlessly explore human psyche both individual and social. They disturb the mind-set of the playgoers and capture their imagination. They arouse a kind of antipathy from the audience. However, when they are actually seen, the audience's antipathy outside the theatre is transformed into sympathy for the characters portrayed and for the life delineated in the plays inside the theatre.

The plays *Silence! The Court is in Session, Kamala, Sakharam Binder,* and *Ghashiram Kotwal* depict hypocritical and double standard mentality of the white collar middle- and lower middle-class Maharashtrian people. In the play *Kamala,* Tendulkar explores the ruthlessness of the media and the position of women in society. The play exposes how man either degenerates woman or venerates her for his selfish motives depending upon the necessity of situation.

The protagonist of the play Jaisingh exploits Kamala's situation for achieving name and reputation and leaves her to her fate as soon as his purpose is served. The questions asked to Kamala in the press conference indicate that society is always interested in victimization of individuals who are helpless. None comes forth to help a woman who is presented in tattered clothes and who is even ignorant of the fact that she is being ruthlessly exposed physically in public—almost in her denuded form. Surprisingly enough, the same society that enjoys the exposure of Kamala goes against Jaisingh, who becomes helpless towards the end of the play.

Both the female characters in the play Sarita and Kamala symbolize exploitation of women—of the former, within the walls of the house, and of the latter, outside them. Jain's remarks about Jaisingh and Sarita throw light on Jaisingh's exploitative nature: "Hi Bhabhiji, I mean, an English 'hi' to him, and a Marathi 'hai' (alas) to you. This warrior against exploitation in the country is exploiting you.... Shame on you! Hero of anti-exploitation campaigns makes slave of wife" (17).

Jaisingh acquires fame, status, and authority in the society. Although Sarita remains a source of inspiration throughout his successful career, he shows total indifference towards her. Tendulkar takes no side—neither of Kamala and Sarita nor of Jaisingh. But the audience feels covertly that he is on the side of

Kamala and Sarita, because both of them are used, or rather exploited, by their male-counterpart. Through the character of Jaisingh, he exhibits selfishness and hypocrisy of the modern young generation, and brings out the oppressive nature of contemporary society. And conversely, through the characters of Kamala and Sarita he exhibits simplicity, innocence, sincerity, generosity, and spirit of devotion of women to their male-companion. That is why Sarita feels sympathy for Jaisingh and provides him emotional support when he loses his job. She is one of Tendulkar's New Women who shows no hitch or hesitation in sharing her husband's concern for the tribal woman as a gesture towards her rehabilitation, i.e., restoring social justice.

Some critics raise an objection to Sarita's sympathy towards Jaisingh with a question: In the play *Silence! The Court is in Session*, Tendulkar represents a revolutionary woman through Benare's character. Then, why does he come three steps back in the portrayal of Sarita's non-assertive character in the play *Kamala*? Towards the end of the play, she says: "...a day will come, Kakasaheb, when I will stop being a slave" (52). Here, she seems to shift her responsibility to others instead of fighting on her own to safeguard her rights. The answer is quite simple.

The characters of Benare and Sarita are totally different from each other. Similarly, the environment, that leaves them to arrive at their respective decisions, is also distinct. Benare remains firm in her decision to give birth to the child in the hostile circumstances. While Sarita provides an emotional support to Jaisingh and saves him from a total mental collapse even after knowing his selfish hypocrisy. However, it appears that Sarita comes to this conclusion, not because she lacks any spirit of rebellion but because her husband badly needs her emotional support. The humanitarian ideology is clearly perceptible here in her behaviour. So far as Benare's case is concerned, nobody needs or expects any support from her.

Sarita, too, it seems, does not change her decision. Whatever she does is a temporary adjustment in order to help Jaisingh in his hour of need. It is so because she tells Kakasaheb: "I'll go on feeling it. But at present I'm going to lock all that up in a corner of my mind and forget about it.... But a day will come,.... I'll do what I wish, and no one will rule over me. That day has to come. And I'll pay whatever price I have to pay for it." (Her gaze is calm, steadly looking ahead at the future. Determination on her face.) (52).

While exploring the complexity of human nature in the play *Sakharam Binder*, Tendulkar denudes both an individual and society. The play is

> a brutal piece of work about a man who scoured the rural villages of his province in India looking for abandoned wives whom he would offer a place in his home, and the use of whom he would take in exchange.[10]

The play *The Vultures* represents a moral degradation of a middle-class family in the contemporary society, and *Ghashiram Kotwal* examines the situation which leads to the creation of Ghashiram-like forces in society. The play *A Friend's Story* criticizes society where a woman (Mitra) is punished severely and a man (Dalvi) is set free although both of them commit the same crime, i.e., the blackmail of a girl (Nama).

Thus, Tendulkar's plays indicate that in his career as a dramatist, he moves from an individual to a group, and from a group to the society at large. The dramatist's success lies in the magical combination of currency and timelessness that are manifest in *Ghashiram Kotwal* and other social plays. Dinesh Thakur, who has directed and acted in Tendulkar's plays in their Hindi versions, makes an incisive comment on the social nature of the plays:

> Vijay Tendulkar continues to be my favourite Indian playwright because of the sensitivity and accuracy with which he depicts social issues. The astonishing range of his plays, be it the victimization of the individual by society in *Shantata! Court Chalu Ahe* or the moral collapse of a family in *Gidhade,* or the ruthlessness of the media in *Kamala,* provides a director a very large thematic canvas to choose form. At the same time, the lack of moralizing gives the plays a very open-ended feel, leaving ample scope for directorial interpretation.[11]

Silence! The Court is in Session is a social satire on the male-dominated society, in which "a woman can neither get a sympathetic response nor win a man to give legitimacy to her child."[12] The theme of the play revolves round the idea of a game in which Benare, who is on the offensive in the beginning, finds herself entrapped in the game towards the end of the play.

The play begins with a group of artists, planning to stage a play in a village. A rehearsal is arranged to acquaint Samant, a local chap, with the court procedure. At the beginning of the mock-trial, Benare is accused of the charge of infanticide (actually, it is foeticide). Surprisingly, at the end, this fake charge turns into a verdict, into a punishment. This very rehearsal of the mock-trial takes a serious turn as the co-actors arrange it cunningly to discuss and dissect the private life of Benare, which has been full of excitement since she was in her teens. Karnik's and Ponkshe's remarks in this matter are full of word-play. Karnik: "The crime itself is imaginary. What more do you want? It's all imaginary.... That's what it is. Ponkshe: Only the accused is real" (90).

In the so-called game, her relationship with Prof. Damle, which has resulted in her pregnancy, stands exposed. All the male-members, Prof. Damle, Mr. Rawte, and her maternal uncle who are responsible for her awkward, humiliating situation, are significantly absent at the time of trial.

Benare, a school-teacher, is sincere in her teaching work and, hence, is favourite with her pupils. She also works in the amateur theatre group along with Mr. and Mrs. Kashikar, Balu Rokde, Sukhatme, Ponkshe, Karnik, Prof. Damle, and Mr. Rawte.

Benare is the protagonist of the play. It is in the light of her remarks that audience studies other characters. All the characters, except Samant, fail to achieve their most cherished goals of life. They cannot understand, appreciate, and share in the joy of others. Instead, they seek a vicious pleasure in making others unhappy. In their verbal onslaught on Benare, who is, by nature, a jolly teacher, their sadist tendencies come to the surface.

All the members in the group, including Mrs. Kashikar, come together to expose the private life of Benare. In their malicious and spiteful attitude towards Miss Benare, their fellow companion, one notices the inferiority complex reflected in their frustration and repressed desires. However, they themselves are not united and share nothing but hatred for one another. While calling upon his first witness, Mr. Ponkshe, Sukhatme remarks: "My first witness is the world famous scientist Mr. Gopal Ponkshe. Well Ponkshe, are you happy? I've suddenly prompted you to world fame, eh?" (80).

During the mock-trial, Sukhatme works both as a public prosecutor and as a defence counsel. As a public prosecutor, he conducts the case very cunningly and illustrates his point against Benare emphatically. But all his enthusiasm disappears as soon as he works as a defence counsel. The witnesses for Benare are chosen from the absent members of the group. Benare is punished severely for her present conduct, which, in her companions' view, is licentious and also for her past life, which is besmeared with sin.

The character of Benare symbolizes simplicity, innocence, and straightforwardness and the characters of her fellow-companions symbolize meanness, crookedness, and cruelty. Her tragedy reveals the fact that, in the male-dominated society, woman's innocence is punished and man's violence goes scot-free. That is why Prof. Damle, despite the fact that he wholly disowns his responsibility, is summoned merely as a witness while

> Benare remains the prime accused, principally because contemporary Indian society, with all its roots grounded firmly in reactionary ideas, cannot allow the birth of a child out of (i.e., outside) wedlock.[13]

The play within the play, which is just a rehearsal for Benare's fellow-companions, reveals the basic hypocrisy and double standards on which our society rests.

Benare is isolated and made a victim of the game cunningly arranged by her co-actors. Very easily they manoeuvre to victimize her since she has no backing or support. Twice she is cheated by her loving male-companions (i.e., once, by her maternal uncle and the other time by Prof. Damle), for they love just her body, and not her mind.

Tendulkar, here, throws light on the evil tendencies such as crookedness, cruelty, violence, that are inherent in human nature. The cross-section of society depicted in the play is white-collar, middle class. All the co-actors come together to while away their free time. However, these educated, civilized people become aggressive and violent against their fellow-companion and that, too, a female and entertain themselves at the cost of her honour and dignity. Benare suffers at their hands for the offence she has not committed. So, she bursts out: "These are mortal remains of some cultured men of the twentieth century. See their faces, how ferocious they look! Their lips are full of lovely worn-out phrases! And their bellies are full of unsatisfied desires" (117).

Benare has her highest moments of happiness, twice in her life, once with her maternal uncle and the other time with Prof. Damle. Having enjoyed "a moment so beautiful, so blissful, so near to heaven!" (118), both of them leave her to her fate. So, she suffers the painful consequence of it. They treat her as though she were a use-and-throw object. Besides, she is, further, ill treated and made an object of ridicule by her companions who pose that they are the upholders of the moral values of society.

Benare has a lot to say by way of a plea. But whether she is allowed to put it in words or not remains a mystery. Arundhati Banerjee points out:

> Leela Benare's defence of herself against the onslaught of the upholders of social norms in a long soliloquy, has become famous in the history of contemporary Marathi theatre. It is important to note here that Tendulkar leaves us in doubt as to whether or not Benare at all delivers the soliloquy, thus, suggesting that in all probability what she has to say for herself is swallowed up by the silence imposed upon her by the authorities. In fact, during the court proceedings, on several

> occasions, her objections and protestations are drowned by the judge's cry of silence and the banging of the gavel.[14]

What Tendulkar explores in the play are the evil tendencies that have taken roots in the so-called modern, cultured society. Benare offers to marry any of her companions but none comes forth to accept her proposal. On the contrary, she is denied both, the right of living (as she is dismissed from her job) and the right of becoming a mother (as the sentence passed on her is to the effect that the babe in her womb must be destroyed). Damle, who is equally responsible for Benare's so-called crime of unmarried motherhood, goes unnoticed. Her fellow-companions give lectures on the dignity of woman and motherhood but they do not hesitate in the least to inflict shame and indignity on her. Benare's tragedy reveals the fact that women are born to suffer even in the most sophisticated, civilized section of the society.

L.S. Deshpande, who has worked on the translation study of the play puts it succinctly thus:

> The punishment meted out to Miss Benare speaks volumes of the ways of our so-called cultured society. The story of Miss Benare's innocence is a long drawn out tale of woman's suffering at the hands of man. As usual, the man is left scot-free and the woman is made a scapegoat by all those around her. Needless to add, however, that all this is just a play and, hence not to be taken seriously. The height of the irony lies in the final utterance of the play: "The show must go on!", exposing the moral and intellectual snobbery of the white collar, educated middle class Indians.[15]

Tendulkar's plays can be categorized as social plays, historical plays, and political plays. The play *Ghashiram Kotwal,* and *Encounter in Umbugland* reflect political reality and exhibit how political leaders render people mindless and thoughtless. Despite the fact that both the plays unveil the nature of the game of power politics, and reflect the political reality of India of a specific period, they differ completely from each other in terms of subject-matters and thematic concerns. The play *Encounter in Umbugland* is a political allegory as the characters represent historical personages and the story represents the political situation of India in the late sixties and the early seventies. It also refers to the emergence of a "New Woman" and comprises, in a small way, and quite obliquely, a critique on journalism. The play *Ghashiram Kotwal* is based on a particular incident in the 18th century Peshwa regime. However, the context is universal, for the characters such as Ghashiram, Nana, and Gauri are symbolic and, hence, belong to all ages and societies.

The play *Encounter in Umbugland* is highly allegorical in nature. Even the title suggests something strange and symbolic about it. According to Manchi Sarat Babu, "'Umbugland' intensifies the idea of hypocrisy. Princess Vijaya stands for the Prime Minister of India, Indira Gandhi.... The play draws parallels between the rule of Vijaya and that of Indira."[16]

The play begins with the announcement of King Vichitravirya's sixtieth coronation anniversary. However, he lies dead when he takes a posture for the painter to paint his portrait. The sudden death of the king rouses the question: "After Vichitravirya, who?" (284) which is similar to the one that has arisen after Jawaharlal Nehru's death "After Nehru, who?"

All the intriguing efforts of the ministers to occupy the throne are proved in vain for the lack of unity. At last, they unanimously decide to make Vijaya the queen so that they may rule the country in her name. Actually, they hand the authority over to her as a part of their game. However, their plans, once again, come to nothing as Vijaya refuses to be their pawn. Instead, she reverses the situation on her advisers and becomes successful in her plan of Kadamba tribe's rehabilitation.

The incident of the encounter in the play is reminiscent of the one in Indira Gandhi's regime in 1971 and the characters resemble those who have been the ministers in Indira Gandhi's cabinet. In the royalist regime of Umbugland, one can easily find the revolt resembling the one by the faction of the Indian

National Congress called the Syndicate group represented by such ministers as Kamraj Nadar, S.K. Patil, Morarji Desai, Brahamanand Reddi, Y.B. Chavan, Nijalingappa, etc., to propose the candidature of Nilam Sanjeev Reddi for the post of the President of India in the teeth of their P.M.'s opposition.

Therefore, Vijaya's victory symbolically represents Indira's victory in the political crisis to see V.V. Giri elected as the President of India. Arundhati Banerjee rightly observes:

> Despite the distancing achieved through the creation of the fictitious milieu, it is easy to identify the characters with political figures who held ministerial positions in those years—the principled politician who spouts moral platitudes; his antitype, a bluntly immoral character; the statesman whose face is stretched in a constant smile and who gesticulates wildly but at the same time taciturn to a fault; the floor-crosser who pretends to be ill and sits on the fence till the eleventh hour. And, of course, there is the indomitable Princess Vijaya herself, the daughter of the autocratic king...who devises her own (successful) methods of vanquishing her enemies.[17]

The character of Princess Vijaya is portrayed with utmost care. It symbolizes the image of a "New Woman." She is one of those rebellious and assertive women who is capable of controlling not only her individual fate but the nation's destiny also. The playwright very minutely depicts the changes in her character from a self-willed and politically inexperienced Princess into an intelligent, victorious ruler. Likewise, her refusal to accept the authority of the ruler in the beginning and her relationship with Prannarayan reveal the human aspect in her character.

Despite the fact that the play is a topical one, it is Tendulkar's exposure of the current power politics. It is through the subtle comments of Prannarayan that the playwright throws light on the role, played by ugliness and corruption in power politics.

The encounter that the play depicts is of dual nature: (i) the one between the ministers and the Kadamba tribe, and (ii) the other between Vijaya and her ministers (i.e., an individual against the group). Under the guidance of Prannarayan, Vijaya succeeds in suppressing her humanity. Gradually, she learns and absorbs all the rules of the game of politics such as "...give some advantages and get some.... A show of sacrifice is always profitable in politics" (306), and "Each of the persons is more important than the next" (299). In her transformation from a Princess to a ruler, she learns that hypocrisy leads a politician towards great success and achievement.

In the political crisis, Vijaya succeeds against her rivals as she takes the situation under her control, brings the crisis to an end, and imposes her own will on her subjects instead of allowing herself to be dictated by others. She is rational, guided by reason and has the capacity to turn the tables on her rivals. So, ultimately, in the royalist regime of Umbugland, the individual succeeds against the group.

The play *Ghashiram Kotwal* exposes violence, treachery, greed, sexuality, brutality, and immorality that characterize power politics of the day. Although the story is based on a historical incident and the characters represent historical personages, the play is not historical. What it projects is cruelty and violence involved in the power struggle of dual nature: one, of the individual versus the individual and the other, of the individual versus society.

Outwardly, the play narrates the story of the rise and fall of Ghashiram Savaldas, the Kotwal of the city of Poona. The humiliating treatment by the Brahmins transforms an innocent Brahmin newcomer in Poona (who has been lately introduced to the politics) into a sadistic, revengeful Kotwal. He has been treated like a toilet paper, a use-and-throw object, by the successful but wily, treacherous politician Nana Phadnavis.

The play is a political as well as a social satire. It projects the society that shields the corrupt Nana and punishes the simple, straightforward Ghashiram. The situation depicted in the play reminds of the lines by J.G. Holland in the poem entitled *True Men*:

> ...the rabble with their well-worn creeds,
> Their large profusions and their little deeds,
> Mingle in selfish strife, lo, freedom weeps,
> Wrong rules the land, and waiting justice sleeps.[18]

Using the historical incident, Tendulkar criticizes society that is responsible for the creation of such people as Nana and Ghashiram. The playwright himself says:

> Though Ghashiram was a product of my reflections on the rise of the Shiv Sena, I was ultimately interested in examining the situations which led to the creation of Ghashiram-like forces in society. The Ghashirams of the world die, but the situations which give birth to such forces recur and are personified in the character of Nana Phadnavis. Beneath the superficial changes in history, the larger dynamics of power are cyclical.[19]

The personality clash between Nana and Ghashiram is the theme of the play at the surface level. At the deeper level, the play explores and exhibits the essential nature of the game of power politics, which is characterized by violence, corruption, humiliation, suppression, etc. Gauri's sacrifice of her virtue brings rich dividends to Nana rather than to Ghashiram. It gives Nana an opportunity to satisfy his physical lust and to establish the reign of terror. Doing nothing outwardly, he remains victorious and continues to thrive. It gives an opportunity to Ghashiram to fulfil his ambition (i.e. to convert the city of Poona into the city of pigs by acquiring the position of Kotwal). The sadistic objective in his mind renders him blind and fails him as a father, as a Kotwal, and, finally, as a human being also. In his role as the Kotwal of the city, he creates a hell not only for the Brahmins but for himself and for his daughter also. He fails to realize the treacherous ways of the culprit Nana and is reduced to a stooge in Nana's power game. In this play, society is shown as succeeding against the individual, as opposed to what happens in the play *Encounter in Umbugland*, where the individual is shown prevailing upon the group in power politics.

In Tendulkar's plays, it is observed that women always occupy a unique position among the oppressed sections of mankind. What Simone de Beauvoir says of women very well applies to Tendulkar's women characters:

> They have gained only what men have been willing to grant; they have taken nothing, they have only received.[20]

Miss Benare, a modern, educated, economically independent woman is capable of carrying out her responsibility, but her co-actors fail to appreciate anything good about her. She is punished severely for the crime she has not committed. Prof. Damle, her lover-turned-culprit, goes unnoticed, unquestioned, and unpunished.

The soliloquy, which occurs towards the end of the play, throws light on the oppressive nature of Indian society. Women have had a lot to say for centuries, but their voice has always remained suppressed either by their female/male counterparts or by the society at large. Miss Benare has been duped first by her maternal uncle and later by Prof. Damle. It shows that men are always ready to enjoy sex with their women but refuse to face its ultimate consequences afterwards.

> The presentation of the soliloquy in the actual performance is the most appropriate one. Miss Benare wants to express the innermost thoughts about herself and the world around. But everyone turns a deaf ear to what she says. So, in the actual performance of the play, Benare's mind and thoughts are not vocalized. She remains speechless. The playwright symbolically suggests the same through the focus of the blue light, cast around her silent standing posture.[21]

Benare is a young girl of character. She embodies love, innocence, and sincerity. Although life offers her nothing but grief, she is optimistic and has a positive attitude towards life. She loves everything, which she is in possession of, viz., her babe, her profession, her pupils, her male-companions, etc., without expecting anything in return. She bears no grudge even against the man who disowns the responsibility of being the father of her babe. Being unaware of the indifference and cruelty of the world, she dreams, almost romantically: "He must have mother...a father to call his own—a house—to be looked after—he must have a good name!" (118).

Rama in the play *The Vultures* becomes miserable for being the daughter-in-law of a degraded family having people with vulture-like tendencies. It is through her character that Tendulkar intends to show that, virtue, if associated with vice, also suffers.

The play *Sakharam Binder* explores the plight of women in all helplessness along with the depiction of complexity of human nature. Sakharam is the protagonist of the play, but the action of the play revolves round the character of Laxmi. The Marathi critic Vasant Palshikar is quite justified in pointing out:

> Actually, the play *Sakharam Binder* is not about Sakharam. Initially, the playwright may have intended to make Sakharam the protagonist. But the play slips from his hand; it becomes the play that focuses on the character of Laxmi, and at this point, she becomes the protagonist of the play.[22]

But appearance is totally deceptive so far as Laxmi's character is concerned. Throughout the play, she appears meek and polite, but at its end, she incites wrath in Sakharam, which goads him on to killing Champa.

> After Champa's murder, Sakharam is portrayed as a feeble character, for he becomes totally helpless. It is a golden opportunity for Laxmi, who takes a full advantage of the situation. Once she gets Sakharam completely into her grip, she begins to cow him down.[23]

In conclusion, it will not be an exaggeration to say that Laxmi has an ambition to exert power and influence over others right from the beginning. The ambition is there but in a latent form, until she gets an opportunity to realize it. Her success in getting entry into Sakharam's house fans the flames of her inherent ambition till it reaches a fever pitch.

Champa's character exhibits woman's torture at different levels. She suffers at the hands of her mother, her husband, her male-companion, and, at the end, her female-companion also.

Both Champa and Laxmi, have their share of suffering sexual, physical, and psychological at the instance of Sakharam, for he gives them shelter and they just receive it in their helplessness.

> Thus, the play *Sakharam Binder* deals with the hypocritical male attitude in India, where a woman is denigrated and venerated as suits the man's purpose.[24]

In the play *Kamala*, Jaisingh exploits Sarita and Kamala for the fulfilment of his desired journalistic goal. Although Sarita is the wife of a reputed journalist, her condition is not far much different than Kamala's. Sarita's character shows women's exploitation inside the family and that of Kamala, outside the family. Both of them are the fellow travelers, sailing in the same sinking boat.

Ghashiram cares a fig for his daughter's chastity and sacrifices it for seeking revenge on the Brahmins of Poona. Gauri's use by her father shows the worst aspect of woman's suffering and man's degeneration in society.

Arun, her Dalit husband, tortures Jyoti, for she hails from an upper middle-class family. According to Ramesh Dhongade, a critic in Marathi,

> In her role or characterization, Jyoti appears rather hollow, loose, and lacking backbone. Through such delineation, neither the socialist ideology nor the Dalit cause is upheld.[25]

Surprisingly enough, it is seen that the character of Vijaya in the play *Encounter in Umbugland* is delineated as exceptionally strong and is in contrast with all the above-mentioned suffering women in Tendulkar's plays. She is the lady of featuring her future. That is why she succeeds in the royalist regime against her advisers who turn to be her rivals.

The protagonist of the play *A Friend's Story* Mitra is a character of a different mould. She is portrayed as strong, determined, having male-stuff, but suffering a tragic destiny. Neither her family members nor her society bear a sympathetic look towards her. At the end, she falls a victim to the male-dominated society. Another female character in the play, Nama Deshmukh cools down the storm in her life by adopting an escapist attitude, that is, she rids herself of the clutches of both her companions, the male Dalvi and the female Mitra by getting married to some other person.

Thus, the reasons of exploitation and the oppression go on constantly changing, but the victims or the oppressed remain the same. J.M. Waghmare is quite justified in his contention that

> Women have been standing at the cross-roads of history for centuries with tears in their eyes and milk in their breasts. Ours is a man-centred world.[26]

While portraying the women characters that play roles as important as men, Tendulkar shows them exploited, oppressed, and humiliated. Even education does not bring any substantial change in their miserable condition, instead, it produces the sophisticated slaves like Sarita, or the social victims like Benare. Suffering is their lot, "the badge of their tribe." It is so because

> ...humanity is male and man defines woman not in herself but as relative to him, ...she is the incidental, the inessential as opposed to the essential. He is...the Absolute—she is the Other.[27]

Tendulkar's plays present life in all its ugliness and complexities. The tragedy of a modern individual, evils in power politics, greed for money and fame, man-woman relationship, etc., are the themes of his plays. Various elements such as classical, folk, modern, etc., have been used effectively. Existentialism and absurdity play no mean, insubstantial role in the making of Tendulkar's major plays.

The existential tendencies are clearly noticed in almost all the plays under discussion. Miss Benare's crazy words—"Life is something like nothingness" (116)—best illustrate "nothingness of our existence" in Sartrean sense; the egoistic Sakharam who is not ready to tie himself to any woman in the bond of matrimony becomes totally helpless towards the end of the play; the life of all the members in Pitale's family exhibits that human life starts and ends in nothingness; Jaisingh's frantic efforts to get a name and money by exposing the inhuman flesh market in the play *Kamala* prove futile; Ghashiram gets nothing even after the fulfilment of his ambition; Nath Devalalikar himself creates a hell for his daughter in his attempt to transform the ideal into the real.

Chandrashekhar Barve, a Marathi critic observes:

> The depiction of life in Tendulkar's plays has an invisible but solid foundation in his philosophy of life. His philosophy of life includes Man, his body and soul, his ego, his associations, the futility in the relations between men, the resultant sense of loneliness, the idea of sin and virtue, the uncertainty of all these.... Considering all this, it can be observed that Tendulkar's plays tend towards existentialism.[28]

The world projected in Tendulkar's plays is a hostile one where man is exhibited as a unique individual, leading a solitary life in the midst of his fellowmen. The protagonists of the plays live a kind of meaningless, purposeless life, but are free to make their choice. So, they themselves are responsible for their piteous, miserable life. The underlying existential principle behind their suffering is: "People are responsible for shaping their own essential being, for creating their own authentic character."[29]

Tendulkar's recent plays such as *Safar, Niyatichya Bailala,* etc., are absurd plays. There is no action, no characterization, no plot. Nothing happens actually on the stage. They exhibit the state of uncertainty, anguish, and depression that characterize our contemporary life.

Tendulkar's plays present the reality of life in all its nakedness. They deal with vices, evils, and limitations in the lives of individuals and in that of society. The dramatist's projection of life at its worst reveals his commitment to humanitarian values at their best. The audience has to uncover the language, so as to arrive at its deeper meaning and significance. To conclude it in Arundhati Banerjee's words: "One can discern, if one delves into the core of the play, the seeds of basic human values."[30]

NOTES

1. An Internet Entry.
2. Arundhati Banerjee, Introduction, *Five Plays of Vijay Tendulkar,* Bombay: OUP, 1992, viii.

3. R. Balchandran, "Foreword", in N.S. Dharan, *The Plays of Vijay Tendulkar*, New Delhi: Creative Books, 1999, vii.
4. An Internet Entry.
5. *Ibid.*
6. Arundhati Banerjee, Introduction, *Five Plays of Vijay Tendulkar*, Bombay: OUP, 1992, viii and xviii.
7. M.H. Abrams, *A Glossary of Literary Terms*, Bangalore: Prism Books, 1993, 120.
8. Quoted from Indira Gandhi's speech used as an epigraph in the monograph, in Asha S. Kanwar, *Ghashiram Kotwal: A Study Guide*, New Delhi: IGNOU, 1993, 1.
9. An Internet Entry.
10. *Ibid.*
11. *Ibid.*
12. Asha S. Kanwar, *Ghashiram Kotwal: A Study Guide*, New Delhi: IGNOU, 1993, 13.
13. Arundhati Banerjee, Introduction, *Five Plays of Vijay Tendulkar*, Bombay: OUP, 1992, viii.
14. *Ibid.*, ix.
15. L.S. Deshpande, *The Limits of Translatability*, a Ph.D. Dissertation, Marathwada University, Aurangabad, 1991, 330.
16. Manchi Sarat Babu, *Indian Drama Today*, New Delhi: Prestige Books, 1997, 109.
17. Arundhati Banerjee, Introduction, *Five Plays of Vijay Tendulkar*, Bombay: OUP, 1992, xi.
18. J.G. Holland, "True Men", in *English Reader, Kumar Bharati*, Maharashtra State Board of Secondary and Higher Secondary Education, Pune, 1994, 174.
19. An Internet Entry.
20. Simone de Beauvoir, Introduction, *The Second Sex*, New York: Vintage, 1989, XV.
21. "*Shantata! Court Chalu Ahe*: A Review", *Pratishthan*, Mar.-Apr. 1969, 31. The extract is translated into English by the investigator herself.
22. Vasant Palshikar, *Sakharam Binder*, *Pratishthan*, May, 1973, 11. The extract is translated into English by the investigator herself.
23. *Ibid.*
24. An Internet Entry.
25. Ramesh Dhongade, "*Kanyadan,* Apayashanchya Maliketil Ek Bhar", *Natyadarpan*, Oct., 1983, 5. The extract is a translation by the investigator herself.

26. J.M. Waghmare, "Literature of Marginality", in N.M. Aston (ed.), *Literature of Marginality: Dalit Literature and African-American Literature*, New Delhi: Prestige Books, 2001, 24.
27. E. Levinas, "Temp et I' Autre". Quoted in Introduction, *The Second Sex*. Simone de Beauvoir, New York: Vintage, 1989, xvii.
28. Chandrashekhar Barve, "Vijay Tendulkar: The Man Who Explores the Depths of Life", the extract is a translation by Ajit Soman and Arun Belsare, in Sudhakar Pandey and Freya Taraporewala (eds.), *Contemporary Indian Drama,* New Delhi: Prestige Books, 1990, 23.
29. Kathleen Morner and Ralph Rausch, *NTC's Dictionary of Literary Terms,* New Delhi: Viva Books, 1998, 74.
30. Arundhati Banerjee, Introduction, *Five Plays of Vijay Tendulkar,* Bombay: OUP, 1992, xvi.

LAW OF LIFE

4

> "...All the world's a stage,
> And all the men and women merely players."
> —Shakespeare

This epigraph aptly illustrates the philosophical doctrine of determinism, which is opposed to the conception of free will. "It is a doctrine which is based on the belief that man's choice plays little or no part in determining what happens to them, since their decisions are overwhelmed by natural or social forces."[1] Man is not free to choose his mode of behaviour, his way of life for these things are decided by his background, surrounding, and other things over which he has no control.

In Tendulkar's plays, the ideology of determinism is clearly perceptible. Most of them are based on real-life incidents. However, the plays are neither subjective nor sentimental in their nature and treatment. In the portrayal of his characters, Tendulkar remains a detached observer. Thus, he attains, in his plays, what Keats calls 'negative capability' or Eliot and Pound call 'impersonality.' The roles of the characters are decided not by will or chance but by the forces of nature.

Most of Tendulkar's plays deal with the lives of the white collar middle class people. He shows something unfamiliar and strange about them. Nevertheless, they are real also. The reality is that man's life is "cribbed, cabined, and confined." That is why, to the question "Why do you often come across the vultures and not the eagles in the society?", Tendulkar's answer is:

> The characters I write about reflect my interest.... Besides, it is one thing to be assured of your security

> and stage a fight against the accepted norms and values and another to fight for the same when cornered altogether. It is the latter that catches my eye.[2]

Man's predicament in this small world is one of the major themes of Tendulkar's plays. His plays deal with the helplessness of man against destiny or chance. So, the picture of life in his plays is gloomy and pessimistic. Man is like a puppet in the hands of Fate, Destiny, or Circumstance. The deterministic overtones of his plays remind one of Hardy's lines in *The Mayor of Casterbridge* parodying Browning's:

> "God is not in the Heaven
> All's wrong with the world."

Tendulkar's plays churn the public opinion as they present life in all its ugly, vulgar, and banal aspects. The characters portrayed in these plays are angry and frustrated, for they fail to achieve their desired goals in their lives—a solitary teacher, Miss Benare in the play *Silence! The Court is in Session* who falls a victim to the excessive physical lust and later on is accused of the crime of infanticide (actually, foeticide); the vulture-like members (Papa Hari Pitale, his two sons Ramakant and Umakant, and his daughter Manik) of a degenerate family, abusing each other and speaking in a coarse, roughshod language, ready to attack murderously for getting their petty desires fulfilled, and tender-hearted, innocent, submissive persons (Rama and Rajaninath) leading a life like lambs among the wolves in the play *The Vultures;* a lustful drunkard (Sakharam) who pretends to be a saviour of helpless women in society in the play *Sakharam Binder;* the women (Sarita and Kamala) who are used as objects, stepping stones or show-pieces in the successful career of a journalist in the play *Kamala;* an over-ambitious father (Ghashiram) who uses his only daughter to fructify his cherished goal of becoming a Kotwal in the play *Ghashiram Kotwal*; an over-idealistic father and his daughter (Nath and Jyoti) who invite a ravishing storm in their lives in the play *Kanyadan*; a lesbian (Mitra) in the play *A Friend's Story* who is punished ruthlessly not only by the society but by her family also.

Most of the characters in Tendulkar's plays have tragic dimensions for one reason or another. However, they differ drastically from Shakespeare's in that their suffering is due to the environment in which they are born and brought up or, due to their inherent wickedness shrouding completely their otherwise good nature whereas in Shakespeare, we see the hero's inherent weakness as responsible for his tragic suffering.

The play *Silence! The Court is in Session* depicts the tragedy of Miss Benare, a teacher. Her private life is exposed and discussed publicly in the rehearsal of the play, which is actually a game, cunningly arranged by her co-actors. The playwright successfully manages to bring out their sadistic attitude through their dialogues, gestures, and mannerisms. Her companions seek a kind of vicious pleasure in inflicting miseries on Benare, as each of them fails to achieve his/her respective desired goals. All of them (both Benare and her persecutors) are the victims of circumstances; and their ill-will or malice is due to the environment in which they grow up or are nourished.

Leela Benare, the protagonist of the play, is a modern, educated woman. She is capable of protecting herself and her child, though her male-companion refused to accept the responsibility. She dreams of the child, who, on growing young, will have a father and a good name. However, her dreams are not realized, all her hopes stand frustrated. The public discussion of her private life is not just relished by her co-actors, but she has also been entrapped in the mock-trial that becomes a cruel, cunning game. Thus, she is punished ruthlessly for the crime she has not committed.

The inability and complete failure on the part of Benare's co-actors in achieving the desired goal render them all frustrated and violent. In their verbal assault on a helpless woman, their sadist tendencies are clearly noticeable. Arundhati Banerjee aptly states:

> The latent sadism of the characters, of Sukhatme, of Mr. and Mrs. Kashikar, of Ponkshe, Karnik or even Rokde, surfaces during the process of the trial. In delineating these characters, Tendulkar has explored

> their psyche to the extent of revealing the hidden sense of failure pervading their lives—the inefficiency of Sukhatme as a lawyer, the childlessness of Mr. and Mrs. Kashikar, the non-fulfilment of Ponkshe's dreams to become a scientist, the vain attempts of Karnik to be a successful actor and the inability of Rokde to attain an independent, adult existence.[3]

The audience feels profound sympathy for Miss Benare despite her unpardonable lapses. Likewise, Benare's persecutors create in audience's minds the mixed feelings of antipathy, sympathy, and pathos for themselves.

The abnormal characters in the play *The Vultures*—the father, his two sons, and his daughter—acquire tragic dimensions despite the negative traits of their nature. It is through their interactions that the playwright throws light on such baser aspects of human nature as violence, sensuality, wickedness, etc. The language, setting, stage direction, lighting, costume, and action of the characters contribute a lot to make the violence vivid and realistic. Sensitive and tender-hearted Rama and Rajaninath become tragic for living among the people with vicious tendencies. Vice is inherently present in each of them and environment adds fuel to the fire. Heredity and environment, thus, play a great role in the growth and development of their mental make-ups and personalities. According to Arundhati Banerjee, the characters in the play are "victims of viciousness"[4] Dr. Lagu, the eminent actor and director of the play, considers them as "victims of cultural degradation of society."[5] In short, they may be regarded as prisoners of their own consciousness.

Tendulkar here exposes the satanic tendencies of human nature through such characters as Hari Pitale, Ramakant, Umakant, and Manik. They are essentially vicious and possess no single good quality. Selfishness, greed, violence, wickedness, etc., are the characteristic features of their nature. Still, audience feels sympathy for them. The characters of Rama and Rajaninath stand in sharp contrast with those of others in the play. Rama's relationship with her half-brother-in-law, Rajaninath is an illicit one. Therefore, it invites criticism from conservative people. However, one has to accept the fact that it is the only humane relationship in the play. Being an illicit son of his father Hari Pitale, Rajaninath is, by birth, cursed. But Rama has to suffer agonies for leading life in the midst of villains. Naturally, the audience has compassion for both of them. Manik successfully manoeuvres to abort Rama's babe, and Rama remains just a witness "Empty of pain,/ And empty of desires" (206). Likewise, the playwright also feels compassion for the wicked and vicious characters, which finds its best expression in the lines of Rajaninath's poems.

The Marathi critic Vasant Dahake considers the characters Umakant, Ramakant, and Manik the victims of circumstances. In his article, he states:

> Outwardly, the characters Umakant, Ramakant, and Manik in the play *Gidhade,* appear indecent, violent, and indifferent. However, they are grief-stricken somewhere in the heart of their hearts. Individually speaking, each of them is hollow in his or her mind. In his dialogue with Umakant, Ramakant challenges him saying: "If you're a man, swell a woman's belly for a change!... No heir to his name" (213). The hint implicit is that Umakant is impotent. Likewise, Ramakant is frustrated for being childless and Manik's love for the Raja does not fructify. The so-called cruel characters are split personalities in that they are grieved inwardly, but, outwardly, using bad language, are involved in treacherous acts. The author intends to show that all human beings deserve pity.[6]

The play *Sakharam Binder* depicts the life-story of Sakharam, the foul-mouthed womanizer. Bitter and harsh childhood experiences in life make him leave his father's house at the age of eleven. Hardened as he is by life's experiences, he welcomes life as it comes to him. Champa, too, like Sakharam is the victim of circumstance. The character of Laxmi is totally different from that of Champa. Hers is a round character that changes itself according to the necessity of time and prevails over circumstances.

Tendulkar, in this play, explores the complexities of human nature. Each of the characters in the play is a combination of good and evil, strength and weakness. At the beginning of the play, Laxmi is portrayed as sensitive, religious, and tender-hearted. She wins the audience's sympathy for bearing Sakharam's inhuman treatment. Besides, she transforms the foul-mouthed womanizer Sakharam into a responsible family-holder. Looking upon Champa as her rival in love, she incites Sakharam to kill her and helps him in covering up the murder. The vicious treatment she metes out to Champa creates the feeling of antipathy towards her in the audience's minds. Thus, we witness her as a totally changed woman towards the end of the play.

The character of Champa is portrayed as aggressive, rebellious, and violent. However, her violence is not without reasons. The cruel treatment her mother metes out to her crushes her tender feelings and further the sexual exploitation by her husband leaves her rough-and-tough. Nevertheless, there are the kinder aspects to her nature that we notice when she generously gives shelter to Laxmi. So, her ruthless murder by Sakharam evokes sympathy for her in the audience.

Sakharam is a complex character that changes with the changing circumstances. To quote Arundhati Banerjee, "He is a man who is primarily honest and frank. His straightforwardness in dealing with helpless women...demands a certain admiration."[7]

Laxmi successfully tones down Sakharam's sensuality, while Champa inflames it. The simultaneous presence of these two women together, who are foils to each other, disturbs him. It creates a psychological storm in his life. The lack of sexual potency on his own part and Champa's sexual association with Daud, his friend hurt Sakharam acutely. As a result, he turns into a ferocious murderer. The changes in his role transform audience's feeling from apathy into antipathy (due to the cruelties he inflicts upon Laxmi) and from antipathy into sympathy and pathos (due to his helplessness in covering up Champa's murder at his hands).

The protagonist of the play *Kamala* Jaisingh Jadhav is courageous and ready to face risks in providing the newspaper with sensational news. He uses not only Kamala, a girl from a rural flesh market but his wife also as objects to fulfil his needs and aspirations. The playwright ridicules the drawbacks of the so-called civilized, modern, success-oriented society, where the youths are shown pursuing their goals at the cost of human values. However, harsh circumstance changes him towards the end of the play. The news that he is sacked breaks him mentally.

It is through the husband-and-wife relationship of Jaisingh and Sarita that Tendulkar attacks the institution of marriage. Sarita, an educated girl from an aristocratic family, works like a slave for her husband Jaisingh. Kamala's entry in her house makes her conscious of her subordinate or trivial position. Despite the fact that she becomes aware of her husband's selfishness and hypocrisy, she provides him with the emotional support he needs so badly, when he loses his journalistic job. But the play ends on an optimistic note that she will revolt one day against the injustice done to her by her husband. On Sarita's emancipation from her husband's bondage, N.S. Dharan comments:

> *Kamala* is a gyno-centric play in the sense that it is built on the metamorphosis of Sarita emerging from being a docile wife to an assertive, mature woman in the end.[8]

While dealing with an incident in the 18th century Peshwa regime, in the play *Ghashiram Kotwal*, Tendulkar represents a *de facto* ruler, who bargains his daughter's chastity for fulfilling his personal ambition and later on falls a victim to the intrigue of treacherous Nana, a veteran politician.

Ghashiram Savaldas, the protagonist of the play heaps inhuman troubles upon troubles on the Brahmins of Poona as a part of his revenge on them. In his transformation from an innocent Brahmin to a sadistic Kotwal, he is used as a pawn by Nana and his lovely daughter Gauri becomes a scapegoat of the power game. The audience leaves the theatre with a disturbed mind, feeling compassion for Gauri's senseless wastage.

In the play titled *Kanyadan*, Jyoti and Nath are seen suffering a lot in the course of their efforts to translate the ideal into the real. He cares a fig for his wife's warning and appreciates Jyoti's decision to marry Arun, a Dalit boy. However, Arun often remains conscious of the hellish sufferings of his ancestors. He seeks a revenge on the upper class people by beating Jyoti mercilessly in spite of her pregnancy. He feels neither hurt nor guilt-conscious for his behaviour as, throughout his life, he has witnessed his mother going through the same ordeal, that is, the barbaric treatment meted out to his mother by his father. The humiliating treatment that he receives from society and the bitter and unbearable circumstance in his parents' marital life render him mindless, insensitive, and violent.

The play centres round the theme of marriage. Jyoti, a daughter of the Brahmin activist couple, Nath and Seva, marries Arun, a Dalit poet. She ignores anxiety of her mother and brother who fear that she will find it difficult to cope with her marital life later. Arun's inhuman treatment to Jyoti, breaks Nath. Her father's former admiration for Arun changes now into dislike. But her physical torture by Arun becomes a routine affair with her life. Her marriage turns into a nightmare. The failure of marriage changes her from a simple, sensitive girl into an assertive, determined lady. She does not give up the chosen path despite the fact that it is strewn with miseries and sufferings. She often recollects the inspiring words. "March on, Oh soldier...one must not turn one's back upon the battlefield" (564-65).

The play ends with Jyoti's accusation of her father that it is he who has made her mentally crippled. Jyoti becomes the object of the audience's sympathy and Arun that of antipathy. The scene of father's helplessness reminds the reader of Shakespeare's famous lines from *King Lear*:

> "Pray, do not mock me.
> I am a very foolish fond old man."

Thus, all the characters in Tendulkar's plays are victims either of their inherent evil nature or of hostile circumstances. Bitter experiences in their individual lives leave some of them frustrated, harsh, and crude, and others tragic. The simple, sensitive, tender-hearted characters suffer miseries calmly and quietly, and the violent, aggressive characters inflict miseries on others as a part of their revenge on society. In the sadist tendencies of the characters can be seen the deterministic overtones of the plays. So, what is remarkable about the plot of Tendulkar's play is neither the story nor the character but the extreme situation reflected in the role of fate, circumstance or chance. However, one may see that the characters are, to use the existentialist jargon, "condemned to be free" while they are facing their entrapment or predicament.

The characters in Tendulkar's plays are types, changing in the course of action according to the necessity of circumstance. Some of them are sensitive, submissive, and tender-hearted. They rouse sympathy in the minds of the audience from the beginning to the end. But even the characters that are wicked, violent, and aggressive win their sympathy. Their fall creates the scene of pathos that evokes the feelings of pity, sympathy, and tenderness. However, in most of his plays, Tendulkar is "able to achieve an almost total objectivity."[9]

It is observed that Tendulkar's plays illustrate the philosophy of determinism. The character's actions and other events in the plays are determined by forces, which are inevitable and over which human beings have no control. Heredity and environment are the determining forces that shape one's nature, character, and behaviour. Such characters as Sakharam, Ramakant, Umakant, etc., inherit barbaric tendencies or inclinations directly from their fathers. The bitter circumstances in life leave Champa aggressive and violent. Miss Benare, Rama, Laxmi, Sarita, Kamala, Gauri, and Jyoti all become the victims of circumstances. Suffering is their lot; they are predestined to suffer. Thus, all the plays reflect the precariousness of the balance between human free will and predestination. They further throw light on the grim accounts of doings and misdoings of the characters trapped in their animal nature and sordid environment.

One can easily notice that Tendulkar, in his plays, rejects idealized portrayal of life and attains complete accuracy in realistically presenting "details of the details." He displays disinterested objectivity and frankness in depicting life as a brutal struggle for survival. He neither praises nor blames the characters for the actions within or without their control. Most of his characters are typically middle-class and working-class people we come across in our day-to-day life. They are motivated by such animalistic drives as sex, hunger, and fear and play out their predetermined roles in an atmosphere clouded by depravity, sordidness, and violence.

In nutshell, it can be stated that Tendulkar's plays best illustrate the philosophy of determinism that was evolved or transformed into naturalism years ago by the French novelist Emile Zola. They bear evidence to the naturalistic philosophy Darwin states in his *Origin of the Species* where he opines that nature selects those who have the capacity to preserve their species and the weak are ruthlessly crushed by the strong and in this highly competitive society, the role of each human being is decided by the necessity of circumstances and not by will or fortune. It seems, this ideology finds best expression in the play *Kanyadan* when Jyoti's brother Jaiprakash argues: "How can the same atmosphere always prevail? Everything changes. Those who are able to adjust to the changing conditions survive. This is the law of life" (530).

NOTES

1. Joseph T. Shipley (ed.), *Dictionary of World Literary Terms*, New Delhi: Doaba House, 1993, 80.
2. Vijay Tendulkar, "Conversation", *Onlooker*, June 8-22, 1983, 43, quoted in E. Renuka, "Casanova as the Saviour: A Study of Vijay Tendulkar's *Sakharam Binder*", in Sudhakar Pandey and Freya Barua (eds.), *New Directions in Indian Drama*, New Delhi: Prestige Books, 1994, 31.
3. Arundhati Banerjee, Introduction, *Five Plays of Vijay Tendulkar*, Bombay: OUP, 1992, ix.
4. *Ibid.*, xiii.
5. Shriram Lagu, "*Gidhade,* Censorship ani Mee", in Narendra Dabholkar (ed.), *Sadhana: Diwali Special*, Pune, 2001, 58. The extract is a translation by the investigator herself.
6. Vasant Dahake, "Kraurya Natya ani *Gidhade*", *Satyakatha,* Sept., 1975, 12. The extract is a translation by the investigator herself.

7. Arundhati Banerjee, Introduction, *Five Plays of Vijay Tendulkar*, Bombay: OUP, 1992, xiv.
8. N.S. Dharan, *The Plays of Vijay Tendulkar*, New Delhi: Creative Books, 1999, 41.
9. Arundhati Banerjee, Introduction, *Five Plays of Vijay Tendulkar*, Bombay: OUP, 1992, xiii.

MORALS AND MUTINIES

5

> The universe, when created, was nothing but the self in the form of a man.... But as time goes on, this self then divided itself into parts, and with that, there were a master and mistress.[1]

In the developmental process of culture and civilization, the natural way of life comes to an end. Biologically, and culturally too, human beings are divided into men and women. Adopting the ways of culture, both of them suppress their spontaneity and lose their real joy of life. They perform their fixed roles assigned to them in the making of an institution called family. Such household chores as cooking food, nourishing children, etc., become woman's sole responsibility. Man becomes the head of the family and governs and controls all its affairs. Ultimately, this leads to the formation of male-dominant society, that oppresses womankind all the world over.

In the so-called civilized society, women are exploited by their husbands in their houses and men by their masters outside their houses. What Rousseau says of man is perfectly applicable to Indian society: "Man is born free, but everywhere he is in chains." This is so because each and every one tries his/her best to suppress others to establish power and authority. Exploitation, dominance, lovelessness, ruthlessness, and violence characterize the contemporary Indian society at large. Gender deformity, power-game, and suppression of spontaneity and naturalness are factors responsible for these drawbacks. Girish Karnad points out:

> I think anxiety has become part of existence today, triggered partly by the endemic violence. In India, the

> more we claim we are spiritual people, the more violent we seem to get.[2]

Although violence is attributed to animals, it is usually noticed that human beings are more violent and destructive than animals. Man gets a devilish pleasure in inflicting miseries on others. The Drama Triangle becomes the characteristic feature not only of theatre but of contemporary human life also. In family system, father plays the role of a Persecutor, mother that of a Rescuer, and children that of the Victims.

However, the large two sections of our society, that is, men and women are further divided, class-wise and relation-wise. Women who are the victims of the male-dominated society become the persecutors of their daughters-in-law, particularly in the east. This exploitative nature of culture is so deep-rooted that it renders all human beings hardly conscious of the fact that they themselves are responsible for perpetuating the oppressive ways of life.

In spite of the establishment of democracy, women are oppressed and exploited more than men. Unfortunately, Indian society, in general, gives its tacit consent to the dictum from Manusmriti: "A woman deserves no freedom." Love of feudal values is a characteristic feature of orthodox Indian society. It is reflected especially in man-woman relationship. Consciousness of personal identity in terms of blood, alienation from Nature, adoption of conservative ways of life are some of the factors that are responsible for the origin, growth, and development of a feudal order. "The programming of roles and works promotes a predetermined, stilted, and repetitive ways of acting life."[3]

Vijay Tendulkar's plays depict the exploitation of men and women within and outside their houses for centuries. They give us a sad awareness of the fact that our love of feudal values is responsible for the oppressive and exploitative nature of our society. That is why, in his plays, he tries to bring about a change in the mind-set of people by shocking their sensibility and challenging the conventional norms and values. It is in this sense that his plays are not just unconventional or original but new also.

While dealing with the evils and drawbacks of an individual and society, Tendulkar throws light on the relationship, within and outside family and brings out their connectivity and complexity. In such plays as *The Vultures, Kamala, Ghashiram Kotwal,* and *Kanyadan* he thoroughly scrutinizes and explains the blood relationship on various levels. The varying relationships in the play *The Vultures*, for example, brother-to-brother, brother-to-sister, father-to-children, etc., expose how greed for money makes these family members wild and mad. In consequence, they become each other's enemies. The play *Kamala* portrays exploitation of wife by her husband without the least compunction. In the play *Ghashiram Kotwal,* father himself becomes an oppressor of his lovely, innocent daughter.

A woman plays a central role in Tendulkar's plays such as *Silence! The Court is in Session, The Vultures, Sakharam Binder, Ghashiram Kotwal, Kamala, Kanyadan, A Friend's Story,* etc. It is through the portrayal of female characters that Tendulkar exposes vices and weaknesses of society. Women are often projected as exploited and losers. That is why, in an interview with Tendulkar, when the critics Satya Saran and Vimal Patil ask a question charging him with an anti-woman bias, pat comes the playwright's plea:

> When I show the struggle of a woman, it is not one woman's fight. The individual must have name and identity and caste and background to be credible, but she is not just a woman on stage, in a particular play. I am, in writing of her situation, showing that the possibility of a struggle against it exists.... By not giving a solution, I leave possibilities open, for whatever course the change may take. When the members of my audience go home and chew on the situation, they might be able to see their daughter or sister in the woman's position and come up with a way of changing the situation for her advantage.[4]

In most of his plays, Tendulkar remains a bitter critic of the institution of marriage. The family system in India is based on mutual trust, fidelity, integrity, and security. However, all these things are confined to women as a class only. Tendulkar's journey in the field of dramatics and dramaturgy from the play *Silence! The Court is in Session* to the recent play *A Friend's Story* exhibits that women always have been treated either as slaves or as stepping-stones in Indian society.

The action in Tendulkar's plays revolves around the women characters. Benare in the play *Silence! The Court is in Session*, Sarita in the play *Kamala*, Jyoti in the play *Kanyadan*, etc., are the characters who occupy the focus of the plays. All of them are educated and sophisticated and, hence, refuse to accept the outdated and conventional moral values and to be cowed down by men. In their revolt against the established values, one can easily see the playwright's social attitude as anti-romantic, anti-sophistication, and anti-establishment. The women characters are treated with compassion and understanding, though Tendulkar is not a self-acknowledged feminist without indulging himself in feministic slogan-mongering.

The play *Silence! The Court is in Session* is a satire on male-dominated society. It deals with the problem of unmarried motherhood. A rehearsal of a mock-trial play is arranged which is actually a "game" cunningly arranged by Benare's co-actors. In the so-called game, Benare's private life is exposed, revealing her illicit relationship with Prof. Damle that results into her pregnancy. Benare is punished without the least compassion, and Prof. Damle goes unnoticed and unenquired even though he is the father of a child outside wedlock. L.S. Deshpande states:

> The play that treats of the problem of unmarried motherhood is conceived as a "game" in more than one sense. Mock-seriousness pervades the whole play. It is a day-time rehearsal of a mock-trial play to be performed at night. Miss Benare, an unmarried grown-up woman, is the victim of the game in the midst of the great laughter, banter, and cordiality. What begins, at the outset, as partly a conjecture and partly a hearsay, comes out, in the final analysis, as the gravest and the most unpredictable truth about the woman's private life. Finally, comes the unkindest cut of all, the punishment that the baby in her womb, be killed, i.e.,

> foeticide (which is, ironically enough, a crime in itself), meted out to Miss Benare.[5]

Describing Benare's character, Arundhati Banerjee remarks:

> The theatre group in *Silence!*...is a miniscule cross-section of middle-class society, the members representative of its different sub-strata. Their characters, dialogues, gestures, and even mannerisms reflect their petty, circumscribed existences.... Leela Benare, the central character of the play is the only exception. Possessing a natural lust for life and a spontaneous *joie de vivre*, she ignores social norms and dictates. Being different from the others, she is easily isolated and made the victim of a cruel game, cunningly planned by her co-actors.[6]

Happiness lies in contentment and greed for money and power leads man towards destruction. The members of Pitale family in the play *The Vultures,* except Rama and Rajaninath, exhibit an excessive desire to have more and more money inherent in the middle-class individuals. In their thirst for money, they do not hesitate to end one's lineage, that is, the forced abortion of Manik's babe by her brothers and that of Rama's babe by Manik. The varying relationships, i.e., father-sons, brother-brother, brother-sister, etc., represent the degeneration of human nature. Hari Pitale, the head of the family, cheats his own brother in their business; the sons beat father to extract information about the details of the estate; Umakant incites Ramakant to go against Rama, his wife, by informing him about her illicit love affair; the two brothers abort their sister's child as they cannot carry out their plan of blackmailing her lover; Papa Hari Pitale, the two sons, and a daughter are always ready to exploit each other for money's sake. It is through the portrayal of such characters as Rama and Rajaninath that Tendulkar provides relief in the midst of tensions. However, they, too, become miserable for living among the people having devilish tendencies.

After the first production of the play Girish Karnad wrote, "The staging of *Gidhade* could be compared to the blasting of a bomb in an otherwise complacent market place."[7] Arundhati Banerjee opines, "Conservative sections of Maharashtrian society were stunned by the open display of illicit sexual relations and scenes of violence that constituted the plot."[8]

Tendulkar, in this play, presents a degraded family of white-collar middle-class people. Greed, sensuality, and viciousness are the characteristic features of their personalities. Manik has an illicit relationship with the Raja of Hondur. She is punished severely by her brothers not for her illicit relationship that results into her pregnancy but for her brother's failure in carrying out their plan of blackmailing her lover due to his sudden death.

Rama, the wife of Ramakant, turns to Rajaninath, her half-brother-in-law, for her husband's impotence. However, Manik her sister-in-law, renders her miserable who successfully manoeuvres to abort her child so as to seek revenge on her brothers.

In the play *Sakharam Binder*, the protagonist, Sakharam is a foul-mouthed womanizer. Due to the bitter experiences of life, he does not believe in the institution of marriage. So, he remains a bachelor. He establishes a rapport with a woman who is deserted by her husband and likes to live with her without getting into wedlock. However, in helping the women out of their precarious situation, he arranges a kind of husband-and-wife relationship with each of them. He pretends to be a saviour of women, but actually, he is just an egoistic epicure. He gives shelter to a woman, deserted by her husband, but she gets from Sakharam treatment worse than that from her husband. He is the master of his house and the woman has to obey his word like a slave. She has to satisfy his excessive physical lust and provide him with domestic comforts ungrudgingly. He wants his woman to serve day and night for him, and respect him, and satisfy him. He cares a fig for her on a personal level and throws her out, when there is left nothing womanly about her.

The play depicts the triangular relationship between Sakharam, Laxmi, and Champa. Their relationship is one of the victims and the victimizer. Champa pities Laxmi and gives her shelter, but there is a streak of contempt in her treatment to Laxmi. However, the situation changes towards the end of the play. The presence of Laxmi and Champa together disturbs Sakharam, who, by this time, grows impotent; Laxmi betrays Champa by conveying to Sakharam about Champa's illicit relationship with Daud; Sakharam cannot control his anger and strangles Champa to death. Laxmi then guides him and helps him in covering up the murder.

Through Sakharam, Tendulkar seems to present angry, frustrated, rebellious youth of the contemporary society. His views on marriage and marital life indicate his practical sense of mutiny against the established morals. He, like the protagonist of avant-garde play, shocks the sensibility of the conventional readers by rejecting the accepted and established norms, conventions and moral values.

Another important fact that the playwright points out here is that women are largely responsible for their plight. Champa shows sympathy to Laxmi and gives her shelter. But Laxmi turns wily and vicious towards her. She considers Champa her rival in love and informs Sakharam about her illicit relationship with his friend Daud Miyan. So, she is largely responsible for the murder of Champa by Sakharam. Thus, Sakharam who pretends to be a saviour of women transforms himself into a murderer at Laxmi's incitement.

In the play *Ghashiram Kotwal,* Tendulkar explores the possibilities of power game. Using a historical incident, he exposes such vicious tendencies of human nature as excessive sexual desire, violence, and lust for power.

Ghashiram, who goes to Poona to earn his livelihood, becomes the Victim of the Brahmins and the prostitute Gulabi. He is put to torture on the false charge of theft and is also banished from the city. The humiliating treatment transforms an innocent individual into a sadistic one. Ghashiram leaves the city with a firm determination that he will come back and turn the city of Poona into the city of pigs. Using his innocent daughter, Gauri as a stooge, he acquires the position of Kotwal of the city from Nana. People who have tortured Ghashiram formerly, now become his victims. Ghashiram shifts to the role of a Persecutor. People are caught and put behind bars without any proof. Ghashiram fulfils his ambition to turn the city of Poona into the city of pigs at the cost of his daughter Gauri's chastity. However, the father becomes a pawn while the daughter is a scapegoat in the game of power politics. Gauri's death renders Ghashiram more ruthless and ferocious. Nana realises that Ghashiram may prove dangerous to him also. So, he uses the policy "to use a thorn to take out a thorn" (63). The death of twenty-one innocent Brahmins due to suffocation in a small cellar becomes the cause of Ghashiram's downfall. Nana, the master of Ghashiram, who incites him to inflict miseries on the Brahmins, does not shield him in his disadvantaged situation. On the contrary, he hands him over to the bloodthirsty crowd. The angry Brahmins shift to the role of Persecutors and stone Ghashiram to death after giving him inhuman troubles.

Thus, shifting of role is a process common to all. Ghashiram and Brahmins of Poona constantly shift the roles from master to slave and, again, from slave to master. The society at large, however, remains unchanged and unaffected.

In the play *Kamala*, Tendulkar attacks the field of journalism and the institution of marriage. By depicting a real-life incident, that is, presentation of Kamala, a girl purchased from a rural flesh market, at the press-conference by Jaisingh, a young journalist, Tendulkar exposes self-centredness and narrow-mindedness of the modern, careerist, young generation.

Kamala's entry in her house reveals to Sarita her husband Jaisingh's egoistic, deceitful nature. He fetches Kamala not to improve her lot but to fulfil his selfish motives. In her married life, Sarita remains to Jaisingh, what Jain, her husband's friend, calls "lovely bonded labour" (17). She is bound to her husband in the wedlock, not temporarily like Kamala, but to slave for him permanently till the end of his or her days.

The play, thus, exposes slavery of women in the male-dominated society in India. Kamala makes Sarita conscious that she is the slave of her husband Jaisingh. Kamala's views on the subject how both of them have to adjust with Jaisingh are like a revelation for Sarita. She says: "Memsahib, if you don't misunderstand, I'll tell you, the master bought you, he bought me, too.... So, memsahib, both of us must stay here together like sisters. We'll keep the master happy.... Fifteen days of the month, you sleep with the master; the other fifteen, I'll sleep with him" (35).

Jaisingh treats both Kamala and Sarita not as human beings but as objects of exhibition. The former brings him a promotion in his job and reputation in his professional career, and the latter provides him with domestic comfort, social companionship, and sexual pleasure in conjugal life.

The play incorporates a bitter critique on the institution of marriage. Jaisingh has brought Kamala for Rs. 250 only, but received Rs. 700 as a dowry from Sarita's father years ago, in addition to Sarita's services as a woman-servant in the name of wife. That is why Sarita, quite rightly, bursts forth: "Listen to the story of how he bought the slave Kamala and make use of her. The other slave he got free—not just free—the slave's father shelled out the money—a big sum" (46).

Arundhati Banerjee, in her Introduction, states:

> From the formal point of view, *Kamala* has nothing new to contribute to Marathi theatre. But the evaluation of the role of an Indian woman within the institution called marriage, considered to be the holiest of the holy in our society, definitely provides a completely novel point of view showing that women are still mere slaves to their male-owners in Indian society in the latter half of the twentieth century...all three female characters in *Kamala* are in some way or the other subjected by the dominant male character Jaisingh Jadhav, who occupies the centre of the plot.[9]

The play *Kanyadan* portrays a middle class progressive family. Influenced by her parents' social work, Seva, her mother and Nath, her father, Jyoti takes a decision of an intercaste marriage. Both, her father and mother, are very sincere in their social commitments. However, they differ in their views, opinions, and approaches. Seva works for the upliftment of

Dalits with a determined, conscious mind. She is well aware of the reality of their lives and, hence, objects to Jyoti's decision of marrying a Dalit boy and tries her best to give her a caution about the risk involved. But Nath hardly gives any thought to the prospects of such a marriage. With her father's support, Jyoti marries Arun and later on faces the evil consequences of her decision as feared by her mother. She follows the dictates of her sentimental father and ignores the forewarnings of her cautious mother, and invites serious threats to her married life.

Thus, the play *Kanyadan* depicts the senseless wastage of Jyoti in translating her father's dreams or idealistic values into reality. She exhibits total apathy or indifference to her mother's and brother's rational arguments and blindly follows her father's path of idealism. Towards the end of the play, her father also implicitly suggests to her to give up the ideals, but she rejects it for she thinks it cowardly to succumb to circumstances. She leaves her father's house with a firm decision never to return and to accept life as it comes to her. Thus, she is willing to rather put up with a marital life of misery and humiliation than forsake her husband.

Father-daughter relationship in the play *Kanyadan* reveals how idealism manifest in freedom of thought and action becomes the cause of misery. The same play depicts the want of harmony in the intercaste marriage of a Brahmin girl and a Dalit boy, who, with his brutal and inhuman ways of loving, sets his wife on torture. Although Jyoti accepts Arun as he is, with all his bestiality, what Arun thinks and says, "Surely we can't fit into your unwrinkled Tinopal world" (513) is an undeniable fact of our social existence. Jyoti's father Nath looks a pathetic figure in his pitiful and helpless state, for he uses his daughter as a stepping stone to fulfil his utopian dream of a casteless society. Likewise, Jyoti herself verges on a tragic figure in blindly following her father's idealism and outrightly rejecting her mother's rationalism.

Both the plays *Ghashiram Kotwal* and *Kanyadan* project the fathers who use their innocent daughters as stepping-stones in reaching their respective desired goals or destinations.

While dealing with the problem of homosexuality, in the play *A Friend's Story,* Tendulkar depicts the friendship between Mitra and Bapu that remains unique throughout. Bapu plays a more vital role in Mitra's life than that of her parents. Her parents never appear on the stage. Throughout the play, Mitra has a close intimacy only with Bapu. That is why Rohini Hattangady, who plays Mitra's role, is quite justified in pointing out: "She (Mitra) cannot forget Bapu because Bapu was her 'Mother.' She opened her heart to Bapu which she had not done even with her own mother."[10]

The play *A Friend's Story* is entirely of different nature. The protagonist of the play Mitra, a lesbian, suffers her lot. Her physical deformity is the root-cause of her suffering. But nobody except Bapu tries to help her recover and change her way of life. Manya Dalvi, her rival in Nama's affair creates a violent storm in Mitra's life. Nama, whom she loves and cannot live without her, goes an escapist way. When Mitra is rusticated from college, her parents do not provide her any emotional support. As she is thrown out of her house, she lives in women's hostel. The play ends pathetically, if not tragically, with Mitra's committing suicide.

The sad story of Mitra throws light on the total apathy and indifference shown towards her by her near and dear ones and also by the society at large.

Tendulkar's plays explore the exploitation and oppression of women by their father, brother, husband, uncle, and fellow-companions. Feudal values are so thoroughly grounded in Indian society that no one can root them out. Women are often the victims of the male-dominated society, as both men and women try their best to preserve feudal values and further perpetuate the oppressive ways of life. If any one rebels against it, the voice of protest is drowned in the noisy cries of the so-called upholders of morality.

> Other may sing of wine and wealth and the mirth.
> The portly presence of potentates goodly in girth.
> Mine be the dirt and the dross, the dust, and scum of the Earth.

—says John Masefield, a Georgian poet. The same idea holds good in Tendulkar's plays. His plays deal with smallness, pettiness of man along with anxieties and complexities that characterize the contemporary Indian society. The predicament of an individual in society constitutes, by and large, the thematic structure of his plays. V.S. Naipaul, in his travelogue *India: A Wounded Civilization,* states:

> An exponent of the 'new morality' of post-Gandhian India is the playwright Vijay Tendulkar.... When I was there, an 'Indian English' version of his play *The Vultures* was being put on in Bombay. The title says it all: for Tendulkar, industrial or industrializing India, bringing economic opportunity to small men (in the play, a family of petty contractors) releasing instincts that poverty not suppressed, undoing old pieties, has become a land of vultures.... For Tendulkar, the discovery of India could be like the discovery of a foreign country.[11]

Human life is always an unending source of material for literature and "literature is after all a mirror that reflects the outer world as well as the inner universe."[12] Tendulkar skilfully moulds the socio-political milieu into the artistic form of his plays. His plays comprise a critique on the vices, drawbacks, and limitations of contemporary Indian society.

Likewise, they express his dislike for hypocrisy, vulgarity, barbarism, superficiality, narrow-mindedness, corruption, duplicity, and treachery. While depicting the drawbacks and vices of both an individual and society, the playwright's humanitarian approach and his commitment to human values are clearly perceptible. They create furore in Indian society, posing new challenges and demanding new morality.

The play *Silence! The Court is in Session* is a satire on social as well as legal justice. Miss Benare is held guilty on the basis of witnesses only. So, the play obliquely suggests that the present day justice is just a mockery. Throughout the rehearsal of a mock-trial, Benare's co-actors try to console her by telling that they are only joking with her. The mental agony she suffers is in no way less severe than the legal punishment. She is punished harshly, even disproportionately, and Prof. Damle, the real culprit, goes scot-free. Contemporary Indian society is still male-dominated, where women are born to suffer. The injustice projected in the play will go on repeating itself in actual life until this "man-centred" world becomes "a human-centred world."[13]

> *Silence! The Court is in Session* is the first Tendulkar play to become part of the New Indian Drama phenomenon of the sixties and the first significant modern Indian play in any language to centre on woman as protagonist and victim.[14]

The play marks a sharp break with the tradition of Marathi plays in respect of subject-matter and mode of presentation. According to Chandrashekhar Barve:

> This is not a play about the cornering of Benare, nor about the cornered Benare. In fact, the dramatic element in it is derived from the situation in which the "being" of Benare is engulfed by the social existence of her individuality. She tries to express her ego openly and freely; and finally, it is throttled, 'Life is something like nothingness'—these crazy words of Benare are good comment on the nothingness of our being.[15]

The character of Benare symbolizes, a modern, educated, but helpless woman in contemporary Indian society. She raises several questions about—love, sex, marriage, and established moral values. Her long soliloquy in self-defence reveals that the voice of protest of a simple, innocent woman is always submerged in the male-dominated society.

It is with the presentation of this play that Tendulkar is recognized as a rebel against society. Outwardly, the play moves around the theme of love, marriage, and sex. But the ideas expressed here are anti-romantic and anti-establishment. The play points out (particularly, Benare's long speech) that neither there is any sin nor any goodness in the society around. Man should disown the established norms and values and move towards a new humanitarian order. What is important in life is one's feeling, one's sincerity or integrity if the life lived is authentic. Benare is humiliated by her co-actors for her unmarried motherhood. Still audience's sympathy goes with her for she is by nature, loving and loved. Benare's innocence is punished, very severely punished by her fellow-companions' cruelty and vulgarity.

In the play *The Vultures,* the aggressive characters Papa, Ramakant, Umakant, and Manik symbolize the tragedy of vicious people and other two virtuous characters Rama and Rajaninath symbolize sufferings of good-hearted, sensitive people. The play indicates the 'no escape plight' of the vicious characters. According to Dr. Lagu, "These characters have no way of escape."[16] Their destruction is at once the cause and the consequence of the cultural degradation of contemporary society, which is really horrible and awesome.

The play *Sakharam Binder* presents the victims of circumstance such as Laxmi, Sakharam, and Champa. Sakharam and Champa are violent, aggressive, and sensual. Circumstances play a vital role in the growth and development of their mental make-ups. The character of Laxmi is representative of those people who change themselves according to the demands of time. That is how, by shifting her positions, she scores a victory over Champa, her rival in love.

It is with the publication of this play that Tendulkar is accused of imperilling the very existence of marriage as an institution. However, growth, development, and destruction constitute the natural process of any institution in the cultural history of man. No literary discourse, whether it is Vijay Tendulkar's *Sakharam Binder* or Bertrand Russell's *Marriage and Morals,* has the capacity to change the social attitude towards the problem, suddenly and abruptly.[17]

In the play *Ghashiram Kotwal,* like in *Sakharam Binder,* Tendulkar once again depicts the role of chance in the growth and development of a person. The inhuman treatment by the Brahmins of Poona transforms Ghashiram, an innocent novice to the city, into a revengeful, sadistic person. His nomination as the Kotwal adds fuel to the fire. In his power-game, his innocent daughter, Gauri becomes a scapegoat. Her ignominious death at the hands of a midwife and the terrible death of Ghashiram at the hands of the Brahmins evoke frustration in the audience's minds. The play indicates that nothing is bad or good in itself but circumstances make it so. The character of Gauri, like that of Rama in the play *The Vultures,* proves that virtue suffers when accompanied by vice.

The play *Kamala* projects selfishness, narrow-mindedness, and hypocrisy of modern individuals. The theme of the play is the sale and presentation of Kamala, a girl from a rural flesh market. Kamala's presentation at the press-conference in tattered worn-out clothes, and humiliating questions put to her reveal the fact that a modern youth is "ready to sacrifice human values in the name of humanity."[18] The character of Sarita suggests that even a modern, educated woman is not so free as her male-counterpart in contemporary society, as she has to follow her husband's whims and caprices in and outside the household life.

Such plays as *Ghashiram Kotwal* and *Kamala* explore the sexual, political, social, and economic exploitation of women. The father Ghashiram exploits his own innocent daughter for the fulfilment of his personal ambition. Jaisingh exposes ills and evils of society, but proves himself an oppressive master not only of Kamala, a purchased girl, but of his wife Sarita also. He exploits her mentally (while providing him social companionship), physically (while performing household chores), and sexually (while satisfying his sexual urge).

In the play *Kanyadan,* Tendulkar exposes the characters that are victims of their own sham and hollow idealism. Nath believes that basically all human beings are good. If the evil tendencies in our minds are removed and destroyed, the earth will be a heaven. Her father's teaching acts like a drug on Jyoti's consciousness. That is why she refuses to take any kind of support from her parents and willingly persists her intercaste marriage although full of misery, pain, humiliation, and exploitation. Thus, the play explores the worst consequences of excess of liberty that render the father pathetic and the daughter tragic.

The play *A Friend's Story* is Tendulkar's commentary on homosexual love. Mitra, a lesbian, is in love with her friend Nama. Nama enjoys Mitra's company but leaves her to face her fate in the period of crisis. Manya Dalvi punishes Mitra for blackmailing Nama. However, in his personal life, he treads along the same path. Bapu tries to help Mitra to reform herself, but in vain. At last, Mitra becomes a victim of the society which is characterized by violence, crudity, selfishness, and duality. Thus the play *A Friend's Story* exposes the society where society does not give sympathetic treatment to a physically deformed person. For example, Mitra here. Instead, it seeks devilish pleasure in transforming her life into hell.

Despite the love relationship between Mitra and Nama forming the play's core, the play is anti-romantic. It is through this relationship that the playwright explores the violence that exists in human nature and attacks the male-dominated society that punishes a woman but lets a man go scot-free to commit more crimes.

The play *Encounter in Umbugland* allegorically reflects the political encounter of the Sindicate group of the Indian National Congress with Indira Gandhi in 1971. It also illustrates the rules of the game of politics, which are difficult for simple, straightforward people to accept.

Tendulkar has tried to bring great variations and innovations, too, in the field of dramatics and dramaturgy. The variations and the innovations relate not only to the plays' themes but to their forms also. The classical, the folk, the modern, the existential, and the absurd elements have been used effectively in terms of dramatic devices and presentation techniques. An individual set against an individual, and also against society, social tensions, complexity of human nature, man-woman relationship, struggle in power politics, man's degradation at the hands of man, suppression of women at the hands of men, etc., are some of the themes of his plays. Apparently, the plays look to be simple, but their simplicity is deceptive. They are rather intricate and complex. In the concluding part of the Introduction, Arundhati Banerjee observes:

> Growth, change, and activity are the three major criteria with which a person's age can be measured. By these standards, Vijay Tendulkar at sixty-four is still a young man.[19]

Most of Tendulkar's characters such as Benare, Sakharam, Arun, Champa are the victims of circumstances. That is why Tendulkar's plays have deterministic overtones. V.S. Naipaul's travelogue is justifiably entitled *India: A Million Mutinies, Now,* for it shows dreams turned into nightmare and reveries into hallucination. The agonies of such frustrated people are the subject-matter of Tendulkar's plays. In his projection of the reality of contemporary life, the playwright's dislike for hypocrisy, vulgarity, violence, etc., are quite manifest. All the plays under discussion dwell on the exposure of these baser or darker aspects of human life. So, Tendulkar's revolt against the established norms and moral values indicates his emphatic demand for a new code of conduct and morality.

While projecting the problems of women in his plays, Tendulkar attacks the feudal values that are responsible to persist with the male-dominated society even in the 21st century. Women are always humiliated and oppressed in the so-called cultured society, inside the walls of their houses and outside, by their fathers, brothers, husbands, and masters. Persecutors go on changing, but victims remain the same.

What is stated about V.S. Naipaul in the comment on the blurb of *India: A Wounded Civilization*, can very well apply to Tendulkar:

> Two visits later he came to write *India: A Wounded Civilization*, in which he recapitulates the feelings that the vast, mysterious, and agonized continent arouses in him. What he saw and heard—evoked so superbly and vividly in this book—only reinforced his conviction that India, wounded by a thousand years of foreign rule, has still not found an ideology of regeneration.[20]

Tendulkar also is in quest of this very vital idea of "regeneration" of man in the renascent, post-independence India.

NOTES

1. Joseph Campbell, *Oriental Mythology: The Masks of Gods,* (Harmondsworth: Penguin, London, 1976), Vol. II, 9-10. Quoted in Manchi Sarat Babu, *Indian Drama Today*, New Delhi: Prestige Books, 1997, 28.
2. An Interview with Girish Karnad, "Where is the Tradition?", *Frontline*, Sept. 25, 1992, 75. Quoted in Manchi Sarat Babu, *Indian Drama Today,* New Delhi: Prestige Books, 1997, 123.
3. Claude M. Steiner, *Scripts People Live*, New York: Bantam, 1980, 196. Quoted in Manchi Sarat Babu, *Indian Drama Today,* New Delhi: Prestige Books, 1997, 28.
4. Satya Saran and Vimal Patil, An interview with Vijay Tendulkar, *Femina,* June 8-22, 1984, 37. Quoted in Asha S. Kanwar, *Ghashiram Kotwal: A Study Guide,* New Delhi: IGNOU, 1993, 40.
5. L.S. Deshpande, *The Limits of Translatability,* a Ph.D. dissertation, Marathwada University, Aurangabad, 1991, 330.
6. Arundhati Banerjee, Introduction, *Five Plays of Vijay Tendulkar,* Bombay: OUP, 1992, viii.
7. *Ibid.*, xii.
8. *Ibid.*
9. *Ibid.*, xviii.
10. Rohini Hattangady, Appendix III, "Note on *A Friend's Story*", *Collected Plays in Translation,* New Delhi: OUP, 2003, 594.
11. V.S. Naipaul, *India: A Wounded Civilization,* London: Penguin Books, 1979, 50-52.
12. J.M. Waghmare, "Literature of Marginality", N.M. Aston (ed.), *Literature of Marginality: Dalit Literature and African-American Literature,* New Delhi: Prestige Books, 2001, 22.
13. *Ibid.*
14. Samik Bandyopadhyay, Introduction, Vijay Tendulkar's *Collected Plays in Translation,* New Delhi: OUP, 2002, xliv.
15. Chandrashekhar Barve, "Vijay Tendulkar: The Man Who Explores the Depths of Life", translated by Ajit Soman and Belsare, in Sudhakar Pandey and Freya Taraporewala, *Contemporary Indian Drama,* New Delhi: Prestige Books, 1990, 24.
16. Shriram Lagu, "*Gidhade,* Censorship ani Mee", in Narendra Dabholkar (ed.), *Sadhana, Diwali Special,* Pune, 2001, 58. The extract is translated into English by the investigator herself.
17. A brief summary of the entry—a commentary on the play—in V.B. Deshpande (ed.), *Marathi Natyakosh*, Pune: Nishant Publication, Dec., 2000, 90, translation by the present investigator.

18. Arundhati Banerjee, Introduction, *Five Plays of Vijay Tendulkar*, Bombay: OUP, 1992, xvi.
19. *Ibid.*, xix.
20. V.S. Naipaul, *India: A Wounded Civilization*, London: Penguin Books, 1979.

BEYOND BOUNDARIES

6

Tendulkar's plays depict the real-life events and incidents of the contemporary Indian society. Hence, there is verisimilitude in them. Most of the characters are life-like. They unveil such baser aspects of man's life as ugliness, crudity, vulgarity, corruption, etc., that are common to all ages and societies. However, the "vulgar reality"[1] projected in the plays, which is difficult for the audience to accept, is not a populist stance; it throws light on the present situation and obliquely suggests the playwright's longing for new morality.

Most of the plays deal with the theme of love, sex and violence. They reveal anger and frustration of the post-1960 generation in the Indian context. The ideas implicit in the themes are revolutionary. They are opposed to the conventional norms and established values. The emphasis here is on human nature and its complexities. In projecting the revolt of the plays' protagonists against conventionality, Tendulkar displays his love of humanity and his commitment to human values.

The psychological study explores shifts and changes that have taken place in the modes of human thinking, feeling, and behaving with regard to Tendulkar's characters among whom we see highly typified as well as individualized men and women.

Vijay Tendulkar, once journalist by profession, is considered a controversial playwright for his plays such as *Ghashiram Kotwal, Sakharam Binder, Silence! The Court is in Session, The Vultures,* etc., as they have created a storm and an intellectual debate in society. At the same time, he has won the highest award in the field of dramatics on all India level for his play *Silence! The Court is in Session.*

Tendulkar's plays deal with agonies, anxieties, and tensions of the urban, white-collar, middle-class people. "...his provocative socio-political plays which relentlessly and ruthlessly explore the human psyche and society never fail to raise a storm."[2] They focus on the conflict and confrontation between individual and society. The angry and frustrated protagonists of his plays are actually the victims of harsh circumstances in life in the so-called modern, cultured society. The anger and frustration of these young men and women is expressed in their rejection of the conventional or traditional values and norms. So, the cruelty of some protagonists is a kind of perverted humanity and their desire to inflict miseries on others is a kind of revenge sought against society. They offer the world a set of social attitudes that are anti-establishment, anti-cultural, and even anti-humanitarian in the existential sense as opposed to the established, cultural, and humanitarian values. However, the world fails to recognize their struggle for existence, their bravery, and their sense of humanity.

While projecting the wrath of the young generation, Tendulkar explores human mind and its complexities in all depth and variety. He presents man-woman relationship in terms of sensuality and violence rather than love and affection. An anti-romantic playwright as Tendulkar is, he projects not love but its perversion, not sex but its degradation.

While pursuing his study as a part of Nehru fellowship, he has won, Tendulkar was left feeling a psychological

> curiosity about violence—not as something that exists in isolation, but as a part of the human milieu, human behaviour, human mind. It has become an obsession. At a very sensitive level, violence can be described as consciously hurting someone, whether it is physical violence or psychological violence.... Violence is something which has to be accepted as fact. It's no use describing it as good or bad. Projection of it can be good or bad. And violence, when turned into something else, can certainly be defined as vitality, which can be very useful, very constructive. So, it depends on how you utilize it or curb it at times.[3]

It is with the presentation of *The Vultures* that Tendulkar's name has become associated with sex, violence, and sensationalism. However, these elements were there in his earlier plays too, but have, now come to be noticed in more glaring light. Tendulkar, who has been witnessed as the angry young dramatist of the Marathi theatre, rebels against the established, conventional ideas and values of the society from the presentation of the play *Silence! The Court is in Session* onwards. The play places him among the leading Indian playwrights and sets him apart from the previous generation of the Marathi playwrights. Thus, he is one who at once belongs to the tradition and establishes himself as an individual talent, a pioneering figure of the Contemporary Marathi Theatre.

For *Silence! The Court is in Session*, Tendulkar got inspiration from a real-life incident. He met an amateur group that was on its way to stage a mock trial in Vile-parle, a suburb of Mumbai. While overhearing their conversation, the outline of the play began to take shape in his mind, and the ultimate result of it was the birth and creation of the play. The original Marathi play was written for the Rangayan at the instance of Arvind and Sulabha Deshpande in 1967, and was first performed in its English version in 1971, in Chennai, and was directed by Ammu Mathew.

The play is a social satire with the tragedy of an individual victimized by society. The brief outline of the story goes thus: A group of artists goes to a town to perform a play. A rehearsal of the play in which there is a mock-trial is arranged. In this mock-trial, the private life of Leela Benare, the play's protagonist is revealed and publicly discussed. Here, Tendulkar presents a world apparently dominated by male chauvinists. However, the dramatic action revolves round the character of Leela Benare. Tendulkar, though not a self-acknowledged feminist, treats the character of Benare with great compassion and understanding while pitting her against the men who are selfish, hypocritical, and brutally ambitious. Leela Benare, who is rebellious and assertive, is a school teacher. She performs her duty as a teacher very sincerely and commands love and respect of her pupils. She is also an enlightened artist. So, she accepts the membership of the amateur theatre group. The other members of the group are the Kashikars, Balu Rokde, Sukhatme, Ponkshe, Karnik, Prof. Damle, and Rawte who belong to the urban middle class of Mumbai.

All the characters except Leela Benare are the representatives of the fundamentally orthodox society. The theatre group is a "miniscule cross-section of middle-class society, the members representative of its different sub-strata. Their characters, dialogues, gestures, and even mannerisms reflect their petty, circumscribed existences."[4] Frustrated and angry as they are in their individual lives, they go to the extent of maligning their companion also, for they are malicious and jealous in attitude towards their fellow-being.

Leela Benare, with her zeal and zest for life, is totally different from them. She wants to share her happiness with others but hardly succeeds in doing so. Her companions fail to appreciate her jovial, generous nature.

Benare, who is far different from others, is isolated. The co-actors cunningly arrange a cruel game in the form of a mock-trial. Benare becomes a target of their gossip and falls a victim ultimately to character assassination at their instance. During the proceedings of the mock-court, her companions deliberately reveal her illicit love affair with Prof. Damle, a married man. The love affair ultimately results in her pregnancy. Prof. Damle, however, is significantly absent at the time of trial. His absence denotes his total withdrawal from responsibility, either social or moral. At the time of rehearsal, the remarks in the book read by Samant, which are supposed to be Damle's addressed to Benare, implicitly throw light on the culprit's escapist tendency: "Where you should go is entirely your problem. I feel great sympathy for you. But I can do nothing. I must protect my reputation." (92).

The court also summons Damle just as a witness, and not as an offender. Benare is made the prime accused for having pregnancy before marriage. The co-actors go on consoling her that the mock-trial is arranged just for rehearsal. But the accusation used for this so-called rehearsal, that of infanticide (to be more accurate, foeticide) turns into a verdict at the end. Through this game, they successfully resort to dissecting Miss Benare's character and thereby unearth her past and aggress upon her private life, for "She is held guilty by the court that asks the school authorities to dismiss her from the job, and further orders that the babe in her womb be destroyed."[5]

Benare's soliloquy becomes very famous in the Contemporary Indian Theatre. However, the question, whether it is a soliloquy in self-defence or a pantomime of symbolic gestures remains unsolved, for whatever she intends to say in her plea is swallowed up by the silence imposed upon her by the court and also by the society at large. During the court proceedings, many a time her denials and objections are seen drowned by the judge's "cry of silence" and "banging of the gavel."[6]

Tendulkar here throws light on the inherent wickedness of human nature that neither allows anybody to be happy with life nor sees and endures others being happy. Benare's companions are themselves dissatisfied with life as they fail to achieve their desired aims in their individual lives. Sukhatme fails to be a successful lawyer, Karnik, to be a successful artist, and Ponkshe to be a scientist. Rokde fails to earn his independent livelihood and Mr. and Mrs. Kashikar are without a child. Through their onslaught on a helpless woman, Tendulkar throws light on their inner sense of failure and frustration. So, the violence that the dramatist pours in words here is psychological. Benare offers to marry any of her companions but none comes forth to accept her proposal. The question is: Who is going to marry a girl with a babe in her womb conceived by one of their fellow-companions? What is more striking is that she is denied both, the right of living (as she is dismissed from her job) and the right of becoming a mother (as the babe in her womb has to be destroyed, for that is the sentence passed on her).

Through the rehearsal of the play, which is ostensibly a game, Tendulkar exposes the double standards of our society. Benare is made a scapegoat and Prof. Damle is allowed to go scot-free quite surprisingly. During the trial, he is summoned just as a witness, while Benare becomes the prime accused. She is not only blamed but humiliated also by her own companions!

"The very men who give lectures on the dignity of women and motherhood are responsible for inflicting shame and indignity on her."[7] Moreover, Benare appears to be the victim of circumstance. In the depiction of the characters such as Prof. Damle and maternal uncle of Benare, the playwright exposes the excessive sexual lust of her male-counterparts. The tragedy of Benare bears evidence to the fact that in Indian society a mistaken, innocent woman becomes helpless and suffers humiliation doubly: first, physically on a personal level and then mentally on a public level.

The play *The Vultures,* published in 1971, stands apart from the other plays of Tendulkar in that it is a play, which displays the unmitigated violence arising from selfishness, greed, and sinfulness. On its first production on the stage, there was a great storm in the society around. The conservative Maharashtrian people were stunned to observe the vulgar reality of their lives presented through the sexual relations and the scenes of violence in the play. It is for this reason that Girish Karnad says: "The staging of *Gidhade* could be compared with the blasting of bomb."[8] The play was bitterly criticized by the theatre-going public. The censor-board, too, felt that it was obscene and suspended its public performance for the time being.

The play is a ruthless dissection of human nature as it depicts violence, avarice, selfishness, sensuality, and sheer wickedness inherent in man's life. The title of the play *The Vultures* itself indicates the unpleasant subject-matter of the play. The characters belong to the middle-class family. Ramakant's and Umakant's greed and viciousness, their father's degenerate nature, and their sister Manik's sensuality throw a glare of light on the baser aspects of human nature. In Arundhati Banerjee's view:

> The beating up of the father by his own sons, the two brother's forcible abortion of their sister's child, the mutual hatred among the members of family underline the fundamental evil inherent in human nature.[9]

The play deals with contrasting situations. The playwright, here, explores two worlds: (i) a stormy, sentimental world that is characterized by greed, wickedness, sensuality, and (ii) a fragile, sensitive world that is characterized by love, tenderness, and generosity. Ramakant, Umakant, Manik, and their father represent wickedness, whereas Rama and Rajaninath represent love and tenderness. Through the character of Rama, the playwright creates a naturally kind, tender-hearted and good-natured individual. Helpless and submissive, she is a birdie among the vultures. Ramakant, who is an extreme addict to liquor, fails in his duty as a husband. Therefore, Rama, his wife, turns to Rajaninath and conceives a babe by him. However, Manik, her sister-in-law, successfully tries to abort it as a part of her revenge on her brothers. Rama, once again, remains as calm and patient as a stone "Empty of pain/And empty of desires" (206).

Rama's illicit relationship with her half-brother-in-law Rajaninath raises the question of morality as she is portrayed as an embodiment of an ideal Indian woman who is religious, virtuous, hardworking, and impressive. However, of all the relationships in the play, this seems to be the only one which, though illicit, is, perhaps the most human. The sexual aspect is so used as to throw light on their love-relationship, which according to Arundhati Banerjee, "is the only redeeming feature in the morbid and claustrophobic atmosphere of the family."[10]

Rajaninath, the illegitimate son of the family, is a poet. His role is reminiscent of the role of the sutradhara or the Greek chorus. His poems throw light on the past history and present situation of Pitale family. He recites three poems in the course of action, the one at the beginning of the play, the other at the end of the first act, and the third at the end of the play. The compassion of the playwright for the victims of viciousness is manifest in these poems.

The play is extremely morbid not only in the portrayal of its characters and their actions but in the setting and language also. The scenes of violence, the open exhibition of sexual relations, and the abusive language shock the sensibility of the conventional audience. Never has such violence been depicted nor experienced before in the Indian theatre. It has stunned the audience and made them introspective.

The language, the setting, and the stage directions make the violence vivid and the play alive. In the background, there are a huge tree having curved, crooked branches and a big hollow, a drawing room consisting of old, unpolished, worn-out furniture, a small country-yard having a *tulsi-vrindavan* and an old garage. When the play opens, there is a constant sound like wind howling over a plain and a shrill screaming of vultures for sometime. When the curtain is raised, the lights on the garage and the *tulsi-vrindavan* are green and those on the bedroom and drawing room are dirty gray, almost black.

The language used is coarse and roughshod. There ensued a long war with the censor-board that asked to omit one hundred and fifty words. All the characters except Rama and Rajaninath are foul-mouthed. However, as pointed out by Dr. Shriram Lagu, "It is the language of the vultures, not of civilized, cultured people. They have to speak only in such abusive language."[11] He further says:

> While reading the play, the abusive terms such as "bastard", "swine", "ruffian", "wolves", "bullies", "lecher", "bugger", etc., appear foul and filthy but, in the course of dialogue, they fit in like punctuation marks! The omission of these roughshod terms will turn the play of vultures into the play of sparrows.[12]

The movements and mannerisms are in harmony with the subject-matter. The characters' way of speaking, their modes of behaviour, their habits of scratching bodies, of thoughtless spitting, of eating food rapidly, and their peculiar dresses indicate their selfish, sensual, and barbaric ways. The lighting technique also helps to make the characters appear violent and blood-thirsty from the play's beginning to its end.

V.A. Dahake, an eminent critic, examines the play *The Vultures* on this assumption: "The characters therein belong to the middle-class society, but their actions are suitable for the upper or higher class people."[13] However, in this play, Tendulkar exposes the vulture-like tendencies that are common not only among the lower or middle-class people but among the upper-class people also. Actually, the world projected here is not one of white-collar people but of high-class, affluent industrialists.

According to Dr. Lagu, the director-actor of the play, "The characters in the play are not wicked by birth. They are victims of cultural degradation of the so-called civilized society."[14] By depicting the tragedy of Rama and Rajaninath, Tendulkar, like Artaud, succeeds in presenting the Theatre of Cruelty. In Artaud's opinion, "The Theatre of Cruelty has been created in order to restore to the theatre a passionate and convulsive conception of life and it is in this sense of violent rigour and extreme condensation of scenic elements that the cruelty on which it is based must be understood."[15] Therefore, this pitting of the two worlds of violence and tenderness against each other is the essence of the play. The tragedy also indicates that the weaklings are ruthlessly crushed by the strong and the mighty in the contemporary society. Physical, moral, and spiritual powers are needed for the preservation of good and for the extermination of evil. Otherwise, the world would be the most suitable abode for vultures only to live in.

In an interview, referred to by Arundhati Banerjee, Tendulkar says:

> *Gidhade* was born out of personal crisis in his life. He wrote it just in four days. He himself was shocked that he could give expression to so much violence. It was a kind of cathartic process. Soon after writing *Gidhade,* he commented that he did not think that he could write such a play, wrought (sic. fraught) with sex and violence, again. But he did. Just sixteen months later, he wrotc *Sakharam Bindcr.* It evoked more resistance from the censor board than *Gidhade* had.[16]

The play *Sakharam Binder* explores complexities of human nature. "Through the character of Sakharam and those of the two women Laxmi and Champa, Tendulkar reaches into the depth of physical lust and violence in human being."[17] The play consists of three acts: The first act depicts the relationship of Laxmi-Sakharam, the second one, that of Champa-Sakharam, and the last one, that of Laxmi-Sakharam-Champa. Sakharam, the protagonist, is at the pivot of the situation. Laxmi considers Champa as her rival in Sakharam's love; the one is a foil to the other.

An anonymous Marathi critic criticizes the play *Sakharam Binder*, in the words:

> One cannot find such a play in Marathi which is full of violence, naked, vulgar reality, and sexual implications. It provokes the audience to think that Tendulkar is the Wycherly of the Marathi theatre.[18]

However, such a comment is difficult to accept. Wycherly's plays reflect the restoration society in England, whereas the play *Sakharam Binder* explores the complexity of the frustrated and directionless young generation in the post-independence India. According to Arundhati Banerjee,

> In the portrayal of this lower strata (stratum) of society, Tendulkar's plays signified a definite departure from the mainstream Marathi drama that mostly dealt with the more privileged section of society. One of the reasons why there was such a reaction against *Sakharam Binder* was its burning naturalism. Here was a raw chunk of life with all its ugliness and crudity which was more than a shock to refined and prudish middle-class audiences. Such a direct confrontation with 'vulgar' reality was difficult for them to bear.[19]

In an interview Sharad Gokhale had with Nilu Phule (the actor who played Sakharam's role), the latter states: "The playwright has suggested to avoid gaudiness in the play's performance and symbolically indicate the presence of the sex scenes. For Tendulkar feels: "If the audience attend the performance for the sheer pleasure of seeing sex on the stage, it will be my defeat as a playwright."[20]

Through Sakharam's character, Tendulkar exposes the masochism of the lower middle class male. Due to the ill treatment meted out to him by his father, he flees away from home. The bitter experiences he faces in his life leave him rough and tough and foul-mouthed.

Sakharam does not believe in the institution of marriage. So, he remains unmarried all through his life. However, he gives shelter to a helpless, deserted woman in the society, not with a view to improving her lot but to exploiting her fulfilling his sexual passion. It is a kind of contractual relationship based on mutual convenience. Wine and woman are his chief attractions. He has his own rules of the game, a special moral code, which he expects his temporary mistress to abide by. The play opens, when he brings Laxmi to his house, the seventh one in the series of his women or "temporary wives" to call them so.

"Laxmi is portrayed as an ideal Indian woman like Savitri in the mythological story."[21] Her husband has tortured her as she fails to conceive a child by him. Now, for her, Sakharam is her husband. She tries her best to fulfil his every need despite the fact that he even fails to understand her expectations and exploits her physically as well as psychologically.

Sakharam's association with Laxmi brings about some good changes in his lifestyle. He becomes devoutly religious, takes a regular bath, and transforms himself into a responsible "family man." He himself notices these changes occurring in him but fails to attribute the credit to Laxmi. However, the playwright succeeds inconvincingly showing, on her departure, the deep impact of Laxmi's daily religious routine on Sakharam's mind through his confession: "There have been many women here, but this one left a mark before she went away" (153).

The relationship of Sakharam and Laxmi cannot last for a long period, as they are totally in contrast with each other. Laxmi is very sensitive, generous, calm, and tender-hearted. Sakharam is very aggressive, violent, and sensual. Laxmi fails to fulfil his excessive physical lust and Sakharam remains blind to her expectations. Both cannot satisfy each other either physically or psychologically. There is no sharing, no harmony in their relationship; their life is totally disrupted. At last, they part company, saying good-bye to each other in a very cordial manner.

On Laxmi's departure, Sakharam brings Champa, the police Fauzdar Shinde's wife, into the house. A foil to Laxmi, she is younger, slightly plumper, and better built. Her appearance, behaviour, dialogues, and even her name indicate that she is whimsical by nature. All good, desirable changes in Sakharam's life come to an end with Champa's arrival. A religious, responsible "household man" transforms himself into a lewd, sensual drunkard.

The difference between Champa and Laxmi is obvious from the very outset. At the beginning, Laxmi appears embarrassed. Although she has been starving for a week, she remains quiet. When Sakharam lectures to Champa in his usual vein, she responds indifferently and asks him to prepare tea. Thus, she dispels his false notion: A woman has to attend the household chores. She never seems disturbed by Sakharam's conditions. On the contrary, she shocks him by frankly expressing her opinion about Daud, "He's nice!" (159). Sakharam cannot appreciate this, but remains helpless. His conception about the sanctity of home ends with Champa's arrival in his house.

Outwardly, Champa appears gross and sensual, but she, too, is touchy and sensitive to some of the issues of life. She denies Sakharam to get into bed with her at the first night saying: "I don't like it at all that man-woman stuff. I had my honour to save" (162). However, she is helpless. For the fulfilment of her bare needs such as food, clothing, and shelter, she has to satisfy his physical lust.

Laxmi accepts Sakharam almost as a husband and, therefore, submits herself to him willingly; Champa, on the other hand, accepts him merely as "her man" in sheer helplessness. She has no alternative but to share bed with him, but, for that, she has to reluctantly help herself with a drink also. Nevertheless, in some corner of her mind she feels that all men are equally bad; a man is, in her view, either a "corpse" or a "dog."

Champa is a rebel against society. She does not accept conventional norms and values regarding man-woman relationship. Her violence is not without any reasons. Her mother's disregard of and carelessness to her and her husband's brutal treatment to her make her aggressive and violent. No doubt, she is naïve and sexy, but her mother and husband are responsible for her being what she is.

Laxmi returns to Sakharam once again. Champa persuades him to give her shelter. However, the presence of Champa and Laxmi, at the same time, creates a psychological turmoil in

Sakharam. He grows impotent. "Laxmi develops an asexual relationship with Fauzdar Shinde while Champa develops a sexual association with Daud", since Sakharam can no longer sexually satisfy her. Though Laxmi finds nothing wrong with her association with Shinde, her moral sense is outraged by Champa's affair with Daud, and she uses this opportunity to malign her rival. This brings out the latent hatred in Laxmi for Champa."[22] Getting his masculinity doubly hurt, Sakharam kills Champa in his rage. Thus, Laxmi, who outwardly appears to be generous and kind-hearted, turns out to be vicious. On Champa's murder, she shows more presence of mind than Sakharam. When the latter fails to carry out her instruction to bury Champa in the house, she herself takes up the shovel, does the grave-digging. Here, symbolically it seems to imply, "She buries not only Champa's dead body, but her uncivilized, barbaric, feminine desires also. Her power to fight injustice appears everlasting."[23]

Each character in the play represents the combination of strength and weakness. Champa, apparently harsh and violent, shows great kindness to Laxmi. Sakharam, though apparently crude and aggressive, emerges a weak man after Champa's murder. Laxmi, who is religious and tender-hearted, turns out to be cruel. According to the Marathi critic Vasant Palshikar:

> Both Sakharam and Laxmi are extremely selfish, lustful, and dominating. In the conflict between Laxmi and Sakharam, the former naturally becomes victorious. The dramatic tension in the conflict is potent with remarkable effects. Throughout the play, Laxmi is portrayed as pious, patient, and kind-hearted. The ending of the play throws light on her real nature. The success of the play lies in its presentation of Laxmi's actual nature.[24]

Thus, all the three characters—Sakharam, Laxmi, and Champa—appear to be the victims of circumstances. The deterministic overtones of the play are most perceptible in their respective demeanours.

E. Renuka considers Sakharam the replica of Tendulkar. From the complaint of his wife Meena, it is noticed that he compels her to disregard her talent and restrict her "to tend his needs and raise his children."[25] Despite his efforts to remove injustice in society, he unconsciously practises it in his own house. In the play *Kamala,* he appears to criticize Jaisingh for treating Sarita not as a wife but as an object. However, in actual life, he himself appears to perform the role showing male dominance similar to the one Jaisingh or Sakharam performs.

But there is no point in discussing all these things: it is an example of biographical criticism; it does not lead us anywhere in the critical assessment of Tendulkar as a dramatist. One should discriminate between the personal or private life of Tendulkar, the *man* and the aesthetic point of view of Tendulkar, the *artist*. Otherwise, it exemplifies what is known in literary criticism as "Intentional Fallacy."[26]

Outwardly, Sakharam pretends that he is a saviour of women, but inwardly he is a reservoir of all that is bad in society, so far as man-woman relationship is concerned. Although he criticizes married life, he develops such a relationship, which is worse for the woman who suffers more with Sakharam than with her husband before. He brings the deserted, miserable woman to his house not to improve her lot but to serve his needs. And he is ready to throw her out when there remains nothing womanly about her. Therefore, E. Renuka is quite right in pointing out that Sakharam's nature is as deceitful as that of a crocodile.[27] Although he understands and supports a rebellious woman, he wants his woman to slave for him day and night, to respect his wishes, and to satisfy his lust. He claims to be the saviour of women by offering them a better life than the earlier one, but he is neither a saviour, nor a rebel, but an epicurean, a self-centred pleasure-seeker.

Sakharam, like Osborne's Jimmy Porter, appears to be the spokesman of the angry and frustrated modern generation. He lashes out at his women and the world at large explicitly and implicitly at himself. He does not care for the world but wants the world, particularly his women to care for him. The want of love has generated a kind of fierceness in his temperament. As a result, he turns into a masochist who seeks pleasure in inflicting pains and miseries on others.

Apparently, Sakharam's anger appears incoherent but it can be understood as the symptom of a positive trait of a character in search of his identity. The harsh treatment given by his Brahmin father, and his running away from home to escape from suffering are responsible factors for the sense of instability that he exhibits throughout. Like the protagonist of an avant-garde play, he shows himself cut off from society by rejecting the accepted cultural norms and established moral values.

The ending of the play is not satisfactory. After Champa's murder, Sakharam is projected as bewildered. So, he cannot follow Laxmi's suggestions. The chief tension of the play springs from his violent, rebellious nature. He is nothing, if he is not aggressive. So, the ending of the play appears to be an artificial resolution. It is a technique called *deus ex machina*, but is used in the way Dickens and Hardy use it in their novels, *Oliver Twist* and *Tess,* respectively.

While commenting on the ending of the play, the Marathi critic Vasant Palshikar says:

> Sakharam kills Champa as a revenge for his incapacity to satisfy her sexually. However, due to the incident of Champa's murder, the dramatic action of the play suffers a set-back and becomes rather flawed and cheap.[28]

The setting is in harmony with the subject matter of the play. According to Arundhati Banerjee:

> Tendulkar is highly realistic not only in the delineation of characters and human relationships but also in depiction of the setting in which these characters enact the drama of their lives. The locale is a mofussil town and the action takes place in a lower middle class home. The extensive stage directions, which have become more elaborate than those in either *Gidhade* or *Shantata* help to create a vivid and detailed picture of the interior of an economically backward household. In their portrayal of this lower strata of society, Tendulkar's plays signified a definite departure from the mainstream

> Marathi drama that mostly dealt with the more privileged sections of society.[29]

The play *Ghashiram Kotwal* makes room for Tendulkar in the galaxy of international playwrights. It proves to be a landmark in the history of the Indian theatre. Using the historical incident in the Peshwa regime, the playwright exposes violence, treachery, sensuality, and immorality latent in contemporary politics and reveals the fact that hypocrisy, greed, and brutality characterize power politics.

The two important characters in the play are Ghashiram Savaldas and Nana Phadnavis. It is through their depiction that Tendulkar exhibits the way in which power operates. Towards the end of the play, Ghashiram is killed at the behest of Nana who continues to thrive. The end of the play thus symbolically suggests that, in power politics, one evil-doer meets punishment but the other goes scot-free. The characters here are types rather than individuals. Ghashiram is the representative of those people in society who pursue their goal unquestionably. Nana is the representative of those people in politics who use the needy people as their pawns and destroy them when they are no longer useful for them.

Ghashiram, a Northern Brahmin, comes to Poona to earn his livelihood. But he is humiliated and banished on the false charge of theft. He leaves the city with a vow to turn the city of Poona into the city of pigs. He uses his beautiful daughter, Lalita Gauri, as a means to fulfil his ambition. By sacrificing his daughter's chastity, he acquires the position of Kotwal from Nana. He, then, establishes the reign of terror; the city of Poona trembles at his name; his cruelty exceeds all limits and the death of 22 innocent Brahmins results in his downfall.

At the surface level, the personality clash between Nana and Ghashiram appears to be the theme of the play. However, the main objective of the playwright is to examine the use made of violence and sexuality in power politics. According to Samik Bandyopadhyay, "In Ghashiram, power is defined 'horizontally' in terms of individuals against individuals; from humiliation to revenge in assertion to eventual victimization...."[30]

In the play, power operates through violence and oppression. In the course of action, it is vested in Ghashiram who does not realize it. From the position of an unknown, innocent novice to the city of Poona, Ghashiram develops into a ruthless, sadistic Kotwal of the city who strikes terror in the hearts of the Brahmins. To put out nails and to wash such fingers with lemon juice and soap, to seal the hands in a bag, to place red hot iron ball on the hands, to cut off hands, etc., are the punishments he has meted out to the people who are caught under mere suspicion. It is due to these acts of indiscriminate cruelty that he meets an ignoble end. He fails as a father, as Kotwal, and as a human being also. In his frantic efforts to fulfil his ambition, he himself becomes the victim of the system. The character of Ghashiram symbolizes violence in power while that of Nana corruption. Nana remains victorious from the beginning to the end. He is the real beneficiary of Ghashiram's ambition in two ways: (i) he has Ghashiram's lovely daughter Lalita Gauri to satisfy his excessive physical lust; and (ii) he has Ghashiram as his agent to exercise his power through. But Ghashiram cannot realize that not only his daughter but he also has been exploited by Nana. In both the cases, the advantage is Nana's. Nana's soliloquy quoted below illustrates the point: "What'll happen is that our misdeeds will be credited to your account. We do, our Kotwal pays. The opportunity comes in the shape of Ghashiram" (24-25).

Thus, putting his gun on Ghashiram's shoulder, Nana shoots at his targets. But Gauri becomes a scapegoat in the Nana-Ghashiram power-game. Nana enjoys sex with her. She becomes pregnant. So, he sends her to Chandra, the midwife, for abortion. In the process, she suffers an ignominious death. She is buried, before Ghashiram reaches the spot.

Gauri's death makes Ghashiram more ruthless and violent. Conscious of the dangerous consequence of Gauri's death, Nana fears that Ghashiram may prove harmful to him also. So, he offers him as a sacrifice to the blood-thirsty crowd without any regret or repentance. So, unabated he continues to thrive. The event is, therefore, symbolic of the fact that corruption not only goes unquestioned, but continues to flourish also. Ghashiram may come and go, but the real power rests with the demagogue like Nana. The social set-up remains unchanged as ever before.

In a sense, the play exposes the close nexus between sexuality and power. It reveals the fact that women become scapegoats of men's lust and violence. It is evident in Nana's various relationships with different women—Gulabi, Lalita Gauri, and the young bride that he marries. They are treated not as individuals but as playthings to be used and then discarded. At her first appearance, he is so infatuated with Gauri, that he says: "Our grandeur's gone, if she's not had. We tell you, if she is found, then this Nine Court Nana will conquer Hindustan!" (20).

Ghashiram's conduct in bargaining his daughter's chastity for the fulfilment of his ambition reveals his "inhuman opportunism" and "total lack of paternal sentiment and sensitivity."[31]

Gulabi's dances, Nana's lustful pursuit of Gauri, the secret meetings of the Brahmin's wives with their respective Maratha lovers—all these incidents bring out the underlying strain of eroticism present in the play, besides revealing the relationship between sex and power.

The success of the play lies in the issues raised by the playwright. The play projects violence in its two-fold aspects: (i) that of the state against people, and (ii) that of people against the public authority. It also explores the varied aspects of the sexual exploitation of women in power politics. The questions raised are not concerned with the eighteenth century city-life of the people in Poona. It means that the play is not topical; it relates to all societies and all ages; in a sense, it is universal. In the writer's note to Vasant Deo's Hindi translation, Tendulkar opines:

> In my view, *Ghashiram Kotwal* indicates a particular social situation which is neither old nor new. It is beyond time and space. Therefore, 'Ghashiram' and 'Nana' are also beyond space and time.[32]

In this play, Tendulkar has used all the three-fold tradition of Indian theatre (i) the classical, (ii) the folk, and (iii) the modern. No other major playwright before Tendulkar has made such extensive and innovative use of folk theatre. The effective direction by Jabbar Patel contributed a lot to the success and popularity of the play. He made use of humming in addition to the songs and music so that the audience have what Vasantrao Deshpande, a classical singer and composer himself calls "the first sangeet natak in the real sense of the term."[33]

The music in the play serves the following purposes:

(i) The use of the traditional songs and dances effectively sets the background of the decadence of the Peshwa's Poona of the eighteenth century.

(ii) They help to provide dramatic relief.

(iii) Sometimes they serve to reinforce the tense atmosphere. Satish Alekar, the assistant director to Dr. Jabbar Patel opines: "After the ordeal by fire the tempo tended to slow down a little. But with the introduction of the '*Malhari*' song, the tense atmosphere, created by the sequence was reinforced."[34]

(iv) The lavani highlights the sensuous, passionate element. It also provides the contradiction in social values and norms.

(v) The juxtaposition of the lavani with the abhanga serves to bring out the contradiction in social values and norms.

(vi) The musical form helps to 'deglamourise' history.

The play begins with a devotional song. Later on Ganapati, Saraswati, and Laxmi come in dancing. This immediately establishes a link with Dashavatara, a form of folk theatre. This opening ritual also has links with classical Sanskrit drama which begins with a prayer to Lord Ganesha. It arouses the interest of the audience, instil a feeling of seriousness and catches their attention. The songs sung or hummed by the chorus also establish the appropriate mood and comment on the action. So, what the play offers is the blend of folk forms with mainstream urban drama, which has created a unique landmark in the history of Indian theatre.

The character of sutradhara is reminiscent of the chorus in Greek play. Like the chorus, the sutradhara narrates the story, introduces the characters, tells the time between two acts, comments on the characters. In the light of his apparently objective observations, the audience can study the characters and also can guess the future state of action.

The human wall, that is used throughout the play, has individual roles. Like the sutradhara, it also serves as a chorus in the play for it helps in the transition from one scene to another. At times, it is transformed into a group sitting in Gulabi's hall, at others they sneak off stealthily as individuals, in a hurry to get to Bavannakhani. At another, it forms a human god-house round Ganapati, and when Nana chases a girl, the human wall becomes a garden. The human wall is also a symbol of secrecy that conceals the various faces of human beings: their hypocrisy, double standards and tendencies to violence and oppression because at the end of the play at Ghashiram's execution, the human wall becomes the fierce mob of angry Brahmins shouting with sadistic glee. Thus, the human wall, with its tremendous potential as spectacle, it performs several functions controlling and enhancing the flow of the story.

The folk form Tamasha is used very effectively from the beginning to the end of the play to expose the social and political evils in society. The play has several dimensions and effects. Tendulkar achieves his effects by the use of the various techniques of his craft. Visual delight is contributed by the scenery, lighting, colours, costumes as well as special effects. In addition to all this, there are quick racy dialogues, often ironical and witty. The songs, music, dances add another dimension to the play. All these are the parts of the playwright's craft.

The play is not so much about the historical personages like Ghashiram, Nana but about the way in which power operates through social institutions like caste and religion to create and destroy people like Ghashiram. It exposes the ugly nature of power game where people are used as pawns. It is for this reason that it is so relevant to our contemporary social situation. It is a satire on a society which shields the powerful and the corrupt and punishes the helpless and the innocent.

Justice is exhibited to be done, and equilibrium of society appears to be restored. The play ends with raising the issues is it really justice? Is justice possible at all in a corrupt social system?[35]

The play *Ghashiram Kotwal* is a classic as it dissolves the boundaries of historicity and eternity. It is the play in which there is the blend of all the three forms of theatre: the classical, the folk, and the modern. It also throws light on the position of the women in the society and brings to notice its worst aspect. The use of Gauri by Ghashiram and Nana and that of Gulabi by the people of Poona indicates that women are used either as stepping stones or as objects of pleasure. The play is considered to have achieved excellence and set a standard in its kind. It is sublime and universal since the situation depicted and the characters portrayed in it, go beyond time and place. The issues raised in the play belong to all times and climes. In that sense, the characters—Nana, Ghashiram, and Gauri are the ancestors of power politics that the world will always supply and observation will always find.

In the play *Kamala,* Tendulkar attacks the institution of marriage, exposes selfish hypocrisy of the success-oriented modern youths, and projects the evils in the field of journalism. The theme is discussed through the triangular relationship of Sarita-Jaisingh-Kamala. The event depicted is based on a real-life incident.

Jaisingh Jadhav, the protagonist of the play, fetches Kamala from a rural flesh market and presents her at the press conference. However, his main objective is not to expose the inhuman flesh market, but to achieve name, fame, and position. For him, Kamala is not a human being, but a marketable commodity that can bring him reputation in his professional career and promotion in his job. Thus, the real-life incident of the flesh market exhibits the violence practised and enjoyed by the present-day generation, particularly the careerist young ones.

Through the relationship of Sarita and Jaisingh, the playwright suggests that, in the metropolitan cities like Bombay,

Delhi, etc., the husband-wife relationship is on the verge of breaking down. Jaisingh represents the typical Indian husband who has no time to spare for his wife. There are repeated hints in the play that the husband-wife relationship of Jaisingh and Sarita is similar to that of master-slave relationship. Jaisingh exploits Sarita as much as he does Kamala but each in a different way. She, too, is an object that "provides him social companionship, domestic comfort, and physical enjoyment."[36] Jaisingh's adventure of presenting Kamala at the press-conference in tattered clothes reveals to Sarita his hypocritical nature which makes her sadly aware of her own place and position as a wife in her husband's life.

While depicting the mental journey of Sarita, Tendulkar exposes the naked reality that wives are exploited either as slaves or treated as stepping-stones to their men's achievements through the so-called sacred bond of marriage.

However, the play ends on an optimistic note. Although Sarita provides an emotional support to her husband, she exhibits a faint hope that she will win her independence in the near future. There is a definite development in her character from a docile wife to a self-opinionated and self-esteemed lady. It becomes distinctly clear, when she asserts herself at the end of the play: "A day will come, when I'll stop being a slave. I'll no longer be an object to be used and thrown away. I'll do what I wish, and no one will rule over me" (52).

The play *Kanyadan* is perhaps supposed to be based on the life of the Dalit poet Namdev Dhasal. It is criticized as anti-Dalit and has provoked a great deal of anger and protest. The play depicts the conflict between the ideal and the real through the delineation of a daughter's sacrifice in pursuing her father's ideals. Jyoti, the daughter of a socialist politician, Nath Devalalikar, marries a young Dalit poet, Arun Athavale, with her father's approval and encouragement. She fails to understand the warning of her mother Seva and her brother Jaiprakash about her proposed love-marriage and the married life thereafter.

Unfortunately, mother's fears and anxieties come true. The marriage turns into a nightmare, as Arun beats Jyoti mercilessly even in her pregnancy. He always remains conscious of his wife's upper class origin. He gets drunk in order to show off his manliness. It is his inferiority complex that makes him restless and gets him sadistic pleasure in inflicting pains and miseries on his wife.

Jyoti marries Arun, not because she is in love with him but because she is impressed by his poems and his writing. It is autobiography that wins for him a good place, position, and reputation in society. Nath also finds himself contented perceiving that his daughter's choice is absolutely correct. But Seva discloses him the reality of Jyoti's marital life: "The truth is that your Dalit son-in-law, who can write such a wonderful autobiography, and many lovely poems, wants...his wife to work. And with her money, he wants to drown in drink and have a hell of a time with his friends. On top of that, for entertainment, he wants to kick his wife in the belly. Why not? Doesn't his wife belong to the high caste? In this way he is returning all the kicks aimed at generations of his ancestors by men of high caste" (544).

The characters of Nath and Arun are in contrast. Arun's brutal treatment to Jyoti renders Nath helpless and somewhat pitiable. On knowing what kind of problems of married life are facing his daughter, he jumps to the conclusion that nothing is real about Arun, his book, and his values. Still he chairs the felicitation function and showers praise on him in his speech in the hope that his blatant lying, his false praise, will perhaps make his daughter's life a little more tolerable.

Nath's blind faith in his values and ideals renders him pathetic. Consciousness of Jyoti's suffering does not make him change his views. No doubt, he believes that Arun's hypocrisy marks a rank opportunist and the devil lurks within that opportunist. Still he thinks that all Dalits cannot be like him. They are aware of what suffering is; they have paid a huge of price for being reckoned as human beings. So, the people who have undergone a lot of suffering will certainly realize the sufferings of others.

Arun has developed the sense of inferiority because of his Dalit background and environment. He is so in his life because there is something barbaric in his veins. Throughout his life, he has seen his father coming home over-drunk and beating his mother half-dead. The incident is carved on his heart permanently. So, even now he often happens to hear the echoes of her broken sobs. Nobody was there to console her crying heart and wipe her tears.

Jyoti has the same experience after marriage. Arun returns home roaring drunk. She notices a savage beast in his eyes, his lips, his face and cannot isolate this bestiality from his personality. He is at once both the beast and the lover, the demon and the poet. These twin traits are so closely bound that, she finds it impossible to distinguish the one from the other. In the course of time, she comes to the conclusion that filthy coursing and physical torture while engaged in sex with her is a part of his frenzied love. Arun is made up of all this horrible stuff and she has to accept him as he is.

Violence is the part and parcel of the day-to-day life in the section of the society Arun belongs to. It is a routine matter with Dalit men as well as women. Whether it is justified or not, it is at least transparent for he tells Seva, his mother-in-law: "What am I but the son of Scavengers. We don't know the non-violent ways of Brahmins like you. We drink and beat our wives.... We make love to them..." (540).

He is so angry with the world that he wants to set it on fire, to strangle people, to rape, to kill them, and to drink their blood. It is his restlessness that renders him violent. He considers the high caste people beasts for treating the Dalits inhumanly. So, his cruel treatment to Joyti may also be seen as a kind of revenge sought by a Dalit on the upper caste people for the misery and suffering they have inflicted on the downtrodden for centuries in the hierarchical structure of Indian society.

The violence projected in the play has three dimensions: physical, psychological, and verbal. Psychological violence is noticed in Arun's cruel inhuman treatment to Jyoti, which is also his way of overcoming his inferiority complex. The vicious pleasure that he seeks from it is shocking. It speaks volumes of the degenerate mode of living peculiar to the Dalits or the backward caste people in our society. Verbal violence can be seen in Arun's abusive, obscene language. However, it is the normal day-to-day language, used by the Dalit. So, there is nothing shocking about it.

The play is, despite its being based on actual life, appears to be Tendulkar's comment on Indian society, particularly on the conflict between the upper- and the lower-class people. Therefore, irrespective of whether he is right or wrong, Arun Athawale may be seen as the spokesman of the angry young generation among the Dalits of the post-1970 India.

The play *A Friend's Story* was based on Tendulkar's story "Mitra" which was written in the mid-50s. The story is related to the life of a girl who lived in Pune, and whom Tendulkar had seen on stage performing a male role. In the preface to the play Tendulkar says:

> I was keen to hear him (her friend) about her (Mitra). (She was still to be seen in Pune) I came to know from his talk about a trait in her that I had not heard of before. She had a craving for a girl, and had an affair with her which ended in a major crisis for Mitra.... I still remember the shock waves and the confusion produced in my young mind.[37]

To stage such a play based on sex-relationship with a lesbian as its protagonist was near impossible. But it happened.

The play explores violence, sensuality, wickedness that reside in human nature. The protagonist of the play Mitra suffers from physical imbalance. She is masculine in her modes of thinking, feeling, and behaving. Even on or off the cycle, she is erect and manly. When her family members become aware of the fact that she is different from other girls, they fix her marriage. Close intimacy and constant meetings with her proposed life-partner cannot stir the excitement, thrill, attraction in her though she tries her level best for that. Consciousness of the fact, that she is a homo and has attraction only for girls, makes her restless.

However, she never remains quiet and ventures upon a courageous, rather a bold experiment with her servant. Developing close physical intimacy with Bapu, she has a desire to know whether her touch can create any sex sensation in him and whether there is something womanly about her. Frankly she asks him: "What did you feel when I held your hand? Did you feel anything?" (425). For Mitra, "Men were good company, but their ways with women seemed weird and unpleasant" (432). The sexual experiment with her servant brings her the sad revelation that "She could never become a man's partner..." (433). So, she tries to commit suicide but in vain.

The performance of a play in her college brings a turning-point in Mitra's life. She performs a male role in the play. Actually, she participates in the play just to while away her free time. But when she holds Nama, the heroine of the play, in a clasp, she experiences some strange excitement. She cannot control her feelings as earlier and realizes that she can enjoy sex not with a man but with a woman.

Mitra remains quite brutal in her relationship with Nama. When the latter cannot meet her in Bapu's room, she grows quite restless. Bapu notices that her face is immersed in pain and she is biting her lips. The biting of lips, gnashing of teeth in the event of Nama's failure to keep her word underline the fundamental violence in Mitra's mind. Dalvi's threat that he will kill her if she brings Nama to the room again does not frighten her. Instead, she stands composed and alert, with the piercing sight of a wild animal. She is, mad with anger not because Dalvi offends her by calling her 'a lesbian beach', but because Nama follows him calmly like a pet dog.

Dalvi's remarks "You bloody lesbian bitch, you! I'll kill you! Aren't you ashamed? You do such things here?" (456) throw light on the fact that Mitra is trying to develop some odd relationship with Nama.

Mitra appears to possess the kind of emotions for Nama which a man is inclined to have for a woman. When Bapu asks her why she does not try for another girl, she answers: "No, Nama, only Nama. Nobody else. There's nobody else for me" (458). It is only Mitra who remains constant and faithful in her love relationship. Nama and Dalvi have just an affair. Dalvi has ditched not only Nama but so many girls also. He himself accepts unashamedly: "That's my business" (490). But he punishes Mitra severely for blackmailing Nama. Surprisingly enough, Nama also does not feel hurt, even though she comes to know of Dalvi's involvement with a new girl.

In Mitra's company, Nama appears to Bapu so happy as if a man called Dalvi has ceased to exist for her. But in her absence, she complains him ironically that Mitra's relationship with her is rather a burden for her.

Towards the end of the play, Nama breaks her relationship with Mitra for two reasons: (i) She fears Mitra's getting physically involved with her. (ii) Nama goes to Calcutta as she knows that her relationship with Mitra cannot materialize and even if it materializes, the society will not accept it. Rohini Hattangady's remark in this connection is very pertinent:

> While rehearsing for the play, I had an amusing experience. To go for the rehearsal, I had to travel by local train in Mumbai.... One day while travelling, a eunuch boarded the train. The train stopped at the next station. A few ladies got down and a few entered. They looked strangely at the eunuch.... Isn't Mitra also different? That look on their faces said so many things to me...while reading *Mitrachi Goshta* again today, one feels that.... The play is of today, because things have not changed much in the past few years for a 'different' person.[38]

Nama, before going to Calcutta, informs Bapu of her marriage as he is closely associated with Mitra. It indicates that she has not totally dissociated herself from Mitra. Although Mitra shows manly gestures in her thinking and behaviour, she has an impressive personality. The boys are attracted towards her. They feel jealous of Bapu as she treats him as her friend. Similarly, when Pande realizes that he is in love with her but, because of her abnormality, cannot win her, he leaves the city and joins the army.

The ending of the play is quite appropriate. It is in harmony with the boldness of its theme. The play is sensational throughout. So, the ending cannot be calm and quiet in line with Bapu's expectation that Mitra will strive to reform herself by mending her ways.

The violence projected in the play is of three kinds: (i) psychological violence, which is projected through Mitra's and Dalvi's thinking, (ii) physical violence, which is exhibited through their actions, that is, beating up of Bapu by Dalvi and Mitra's attempt to strangle Nama, and (iii) verbal violence, which, is perceptible through some coarse, roughshod dialogues of the characters. The play explores the nature of both homosexual and heterosexual love. However, the play's main focus is the projection of violence: the violence that exists in a sexually perverted or deformed person and the psychic violence that society callously exhibits towards such an individual. Dalvi symbolically represents the kind of violence society inflicts on the individual who, by nature, happens to be harmless and helpless.

The adept handling of such 'forbidden' subject-matter, once again, proves the fact that Tendulkar is an avant-garde playwright.

Tendulkar's plays span varied issues which explain their appeal to a cross-section of society from *Kamala* which attacks the media's credo of "anything for a good story", to *Mitrachi Gosht* which takes a bold look at hetero and homosexual love.[39] He is the Osborne of Indian theatre as his play *Silence! The Court is in Session* heralds the beginning of "New Drama." The protagonist of the play, Leela Benare, like Ibsen's Nora, challenges the outdated customs and traditions, and his Sakharam, like Osborne's Jimmy, is a spokesman of the angry and frustrated post-1970 generation.

In most of his plays, Tendulkar highlights woman's suffering and senseless wastage because of brutal, irresponsible behaviour of man. However, he neither praises, nor condemns men as well as women. But he has a silent sympathy for women who suffer at the expense of men. He is highly objective and incisive in his criticism of life and society.

To illustrate the point, one sees that Benare falls a victim to infatuation and excessive physical lust of the two male culprits—the one is her maternal uncle and the other an intellectual companion. She falls not due to any of her weaknesses but due to her excessive simplicity and sheer innocence. Rama's condition is like a helpless, tender, little bird among the vultures. Champa, who appears outwardly rebellious, is ruthlessly crushed as she fails to understand hatred and jealousy of her apparently weak but sensitive female companion. Kamala and Sarita both become the stepping-stones to their respective man's achievement. The play *Ghashiram Kotwal* depicts the sacrifice of a daughter for the ambition of her father to become the Kotwal of the city of Poona and the play *Kanyadan* deals with the sacrifice of a daughter for the fulfilment of her father's ambition to become a social reformer.

Thus, all the plays describe violence, power, repression, and frustration that exist in the contemporary Indian society. Violence is noticed everywhere in Tendulkar's dramatic world—in the cruel, cunning game in the form of a mock-trial in *Silence! The Court is in Session,* in an over-ambitious young journalist's craze for money and fame in *Kamala*, in excessive sexual lust of the protagonist in *Sakharam Binder,* in the rude, brutal interactions of the family members in *The Vultures*, in Ghashiram's revenge on the Brahmins of Poona and *vice versa* in *Ghashiram Kotwal*, in a young Dalit's brutal treatment of his pregnant wife in *Kanyadan*, and finally, in Mitra's relationship to Nama in *A Friend's Story*. Therefore, "all these plays are, in fact, spectacles of violence, overt or covert."[40]

NOTES

1. Arundhati Banerjee, Introduction, *Five Plays of Vijay Tendulkar*, Bombay: OUP, 1992, xv.
2. An Internet Entry.
3. Vijay Tendulkar, interviewed by Elizabeth Roy, in *Indian Review of Books,* Vol. 2, No. 7, April-May, 1993. Quoted by Samik Bandyopadhyay, Introduction, *Collected Plays in Translation*, New Delhi: OUP, 2002, xli-xlii.
4. Arundhati Banerjee, Introduction, *Five Plays of Vijay Tendulkar*, Bombay: OUP, 1992, viii.

5. Geeta Kumar, "Portrayal of Women in Tendulkar's *Shantata! Court Chalu Ahe* and *Sakharam Binder*", in Sudhakar Pandey and Freya Barua (eds.), *New Directions in Indian Drama,* New Delhi: Prestige Books, 1994, 24.
6. Arundhati Banerjee, Introduction, *Five Plays of Vijay Tendulkar*, Bombay: OUP, 1992, ix.
7. V.N. Dass, "Women Characters in the Plays of Vijay Tendulkar", in Sudhakar Pandey and Freya Barua (eds.), *New Directions in Indian Drama*, New Delhi: Prestige Books, 1994, 12.
8. Arundhati Banerjee, Introduction, *Five Plays of Vijay Tendulkar*, Bombay: OUP, 1992, xii.
9. *Ibid.*
10. *Ibid.*, xiii.
11. Shriram Lagu, "*Gidhade*, Censorship ani Mee", in Narendra Dabholkar (ed.), *Sadhana: Diwali Special,* Pune, 2001, 55. The extract is translated into English by the investigator herself.
12. *Ibid.*, 55, 57.
13. Vasant Dahake, "Krauryanatya ani *Gidhade*", *Satyakatha*, Sept., 1995, 12-13. The extract is translated into English by the investigator.
14. Shriram Lagu, "*Gidhade*, Censorship ani Mee", in Narendra Dabholkar (ed.), *Sadhana: Diwali Special,* Pune, 2001, 58. The extract is a translation in English by the investigator herself.
15. Eric Beautely (ed.), "The Theory of the Modern Stage", London: Penguin, 1983, 66. Quoted in Asha S. Kanwar, *Ghashiram Kotwal: A Study Guide,* New Delhi: IGNOU, 1993, 50.
16. Arundhati Banerjee, Introduction, *Five Plays of Vijay Tendulkar*, Bombay: OUP, 1992, xv.
17. An Internet Entry.
18. "Wadagrasta Tharalele Natak *Sakharam Binder*: Vijay Tendulkar", 1972, 18-19, *Alochana*, Pune: Nilkanth Publication. The extract is translated into English by the investigator herself.
19. Arundhati Banerjee, Introduction, *Five Plays of Vijay Tendulkar,* Bombay: OUP, 1992, xv.
20. "Nilu Phule: Mulakhat: Sharad Gokhle", *Kesari*: Sunday, May 7, 1972, 11, Translated into English by the investigator herself.
21. Veena Noble Dass, "Women Characters in the Plays of Vijay Tendulkar", in Sudhakar Pandey and Freya Barua (eds.), *New Directions in Indian Drama,* New Delhi: Prestige Books, 1994, 12.
22. Arundhati Banerjee, Introduction, *Five Plays of Vijay Tendulkar*, Bombay: OUP, 1992, xv.
23. Tara Bhawalkar, *Marathi Natak—Nawya Disha, Nawi Walne,* Pune: Mehta Publication House, 1997, 73. The extract is translated into English by the research worker herself.

24. Vasant Palshikar, *Sakharam Binder*, *Pratishthan*, May, 1973, 17. The extract is translated into English by the investigator herself.
25. E. Renuka, "Casanova as the Saviour: A Study of Vijay Tendulkar's *Sakharam Binder*", in Sudhakar Pandey and Freya Barua (eds.), *New Directions in Indian Drama,* New Delhi: Prestige Books, 1994, 33.
26. M.H. Abrams, *A Glossary of Literary Terms,* Bangalore: Prism Books, 1993, 90.
27. E. Renuka, "Casanova as the Saviour: A Study of Vijay Tendulkar's *Sakharam Binder*", in Sudhakar Pandey and Freya Barua (eds.), *New Directions in Indian Drama,* New Delhi: Prestige Books, 1994, 35.
28. Vasant Palshikar, *Sakharam Binder*, *Pratishthan*, May, 1973, 11. The extract is a translation by the investigator herself.
29. Arundhati Banerjee, Introduction, *Five Plays of Vijay Tendulkar*, Bombay: OUP, 1992, xv.
30. Samik Bandyopadhyay, Introduction, Vijay Tendulkar, *Ghashiram Kotwal*, translated by Jayant Karve and Eleanor Zelliot, Calcutta: Seagull, 1984, 3.
31. Asha S. Kanwar, *Ghashiram Kotwal: A Study Guide,* New Delhi: IGNOU, 1993, 31.
32. *Ibid.*, 18.
33. In Pushpa Bhave, 'Contemporary Indian Theatre: Interviews with Playwrights and Directors' (New Delhi: Sangeet Natak Akademi), 1989, 47.
34. *Ghashiram Kotwal*: A Production Casebook, Ghashiram Kotwal, xiv-xv.
35. Asha S. Kanwar, *Ghashiram Kotwal: A Study Guide*, New Delhi: IGNOU, 1993, 20.
36. Arundhati Banerjee, Introduction, *Five Plays of Vijay Tendulkar*, Bombay: OUP, 1992, xvii.
37. Vijay Tendulkar, Preface, *A Friend's Story,* New Delhi: OUP, 2001, quoted again in Preface, *Collected Plays in Translation*, New Delhi: OUP, 2003, XV.
38. Rohini Hattangady, Appendix III, "Note on *A Friend's Story*", *Collected Plays in Translation*, OUP, 2003, 569.
39. An Internet Entry.
40. N.S. Dharan, *The Plays of Vijay Tendulkar*, New Delhi: Creative Books, 1999, 107.

BODY AND SOUL

7

Viewed chronologically, primitivism signifies a view that an ideal era of human life existed in the distant past and that the process of history has been the chronological decline from a natural, blissful, innocent state to the present state of increasing complexity, artificiality, and anxiety. Cultural primitivism indicates that primitive man is better than his civilized counterpart and that primitive life is superior to the civilized one. The term "deformity", reflects in more than one aspect or dimension a sequence to and an extension of the distorted state of our civilization. Distortion implies deviation from norm. It means something abnormal, a sense of being crippled.

While commenting on Tendulkar's play *Silence! The Court is in Session,* G.P. Deshpande asserts:

> Modernization costs the loss of individual freedom. In Freud's words, civilization comes into being from the suppression of Eros.... From conceptual point of view we think true, ideal individual freedom thrives only in the civilized world, but actually, in practice, it implies that we should put up with tyranny.[1]

With the march of progressive civilization, the natural way of life comes to an end. Culture distorts human personality. As a result of distortion, everyone acquires a deformed personality. Badal Sircar makes a point in saying: "I am a fragmented man living in a fragmented world full of contradictions."[2]

There are six modes or dimensions of deformity as indicated below: (i) The sex role attributed to human beings causes gender deformity. (ii) The division of society on the basis of caste, class, colour, and religion is the cause of social deformity. (iii) In the economically divided society, the poor suffer from inferiority complex and the rich from superiority complex. Responding to these complexes, they play power games and manifest political deformity. (iv) Inequality of justice invades human mind and makes him mentally deformed. (v) Similarly, heredity and environment affect his physique and render him physically deformed. (vi) The cut-throat competition for fame, money, and position in the hierarchical society dehumanizes man. It cripples his soul and makes him loveless. This process of dehumanization finally culminates in his spiritual deformity. It paves way for man's self-destruction and self-annihilation.

The plays of Tendulkar variously deal with the different dimensions of man's cultural deformity and bring out its evil consequences on human body, mind, and spirit.

Biologically as well as culturally, human beings are divided into two classes: men and women. This division is further accentuated by the roles they are assigned to play in the making of family. Man is the head of the family, governing and controlling all its affairs. Woman is entrusted with the household responsibilities, particularly those of cooking food and rearing children. This leads to the formation of exploitative and oppressive society of men as against the exploited and oppressed society of women. Simone de Beauvoir rightly observes: "One is not born but rather becomes a woman.... It is civilization as whole that produces this culture...which is described as feminine."[3]

Vijay Tendulkar deals with the theme of gender deformity in his plays. It is noticeable in almost all the plays. However, it is explored more deeply and more elaborately in the play *Kamala*. Using a real-life incident, Tendulkar highlights the position of women in the success-oriented, male-dominated Indian society. The triangular relationship of Sarita-Jaisingh-Kamala exposes the oppressive modern society where housewives like Sarita are exploited inside their houses by their husbands, and men, too, are exploited outside their houses by their masters or employers.

Jaisingh works very sincerely for his employer and Sarita for her husband. He used to take risks to expose evils and drawbacks in society. Sarita, too, takes care of his needs at home as jotting down the telephonic messages, keeping delicious food and drinks ready for him. She does all these things promptly to keep her husband refreshed so that he may work efficiently.

Despite the fact that Sarita and Jaisingh are both devoted to their respective causes, there is a lot of difference in their spirit of devotion. Jaisingh works aspiring for money, reputation, and fame. Sarita works for her husband's pleasure and satisfaction without any personal self-interest or ulterior motive.

Jaisingh buys Kamala from a rural flesh market for Rs. 250. Inspite of the warning of Kakasaheb: "You may be caught in a terrible jam some time" (10), he decides to present her at the press conference not with a view to exposing the inhuman flesh market but as a part of his professional commitment. For Jaisingh, Kamala is a key to his successful career and the bright, glorious future that lies ahead of him.

In the press conference, which is outwardly held to expose the sexual harassment of the helpless woman Kamala is exposed physically and psychologically. She is presented in tattered clothes and has to answer unpleasant queries such as: "If there is a free sex among you, what do you do with the illegitimate children? How many men have you slept with?" (29). Kamala feels embarrassed, while Jaisingh and his friend Jain, flushed with wine, enjoy themselves. Greed for money and craze for success render Jaisingh loveless and mindless.

The relationship of Jaisingh and Sarita in the play is similar to that of persecutor-victim relationship. Arundhati Banerjee rightly points out:

> Like Kamala, Sarita too, is an object of Jaisingh's life, an object that provides him domestic comfort, social companionship, and sexual pleasure.... She, too, in her own way, is as exploited as Kamala. Kamala's entry into the household reveals to Sarita the selfish hypocrisy of her husband and the insignificance of her own existence.[4]

Kamala's innocent question: "How much did he buy you for?" (34) makes Sarita introspective. For Kamala, Jaisingh pays Rs. 250 whereas for Sarita, he is paid Rs. 700 as dowry. Thus, both of them are "objects" of pleasure, money, and reputation. That is why Jaisingh's arrogant remark—"It's I who take decisions in this house and no one else" (42)—makes her realize that he is the master and she the slave. Jaisingh is the best example of what an Indian husband is to his wife.

By introducing the character of Kakasaheb, Tendulkar throws light not only on the true ideals of journalism but also on the exploitation of women in society for centuries. It is noticed when Kakasaheb tries to cool down Sarita by telling: "I gave your aunt a lot of trouble. As if it was my right. I did not care what she felt at all" (47).

Despite the fact that the play *Kamala* presents a critique of the male-dominated society, it indirectly illustrates another important aspect of society that women themselves are responsible for their exploitation. Sarita becomes conscious of the hypocritical nature of her husband. Still she provides him an emotional support, when he loses his job towards the end of the play. The character of Kamala represents an illiterate, unconscious slave in the flesh market and that of Sarita represents an educated, sophisticated slave in the household. Both of them lack the guts and the courage to rebel against injustice. Therefore, they cannot help becoming scapegoats as if in the conspiracy of their male-counterparts.

Likewise, Tendulkar's other plays such as *Silence! The Court is in Session*, *Sakharam Binder, The Vultures, Ghashiram Kotwal,* and *Kanyadan* deal with the theme of gender deformity. They represent how the present society lacks in what we call poetic justice. It is the society where virtue is born to suffer. Everybody fails to appreciate Benare's sheer innocence and her feeling of genuine love; Champa, though apparently strong and aggressive, is victimized not only by her male-companion Sakharam but by her female-companion Laxmi also; the entire life becomes a punishment for Rama, since she has to lead her life in the company of vulture-like people; Gauri is made a scapegoat by her own father Ghashiram; Jyoti in *Kanyadan* has to suffer inhuman troubles at the instance of her Dalit husband as a part of his revenge on the upper middle-class society.

All these plays illustrate, more or less, how women are exploited in various ways. The inhuman treatment that they receive from the male-dominated society indicates that they lose their freedom first and their lives later for the sake of man. Ideally speaking, it is sacrifice, but as Tendulkar is a realist, he sees it as sheer wastage on the part of Indian women.

Exploitation and oppression are the characteristic features of Indian society for centuries. The whole society is divided on the basis of caste, class, religion, sex, and colour. The division is culturally programmed in the form of caste-system and varna-system and as such is transmitted from generation to generation. All this leads to social deformity. Such novelists as Mulk Raj Anand, Khushwant Singh, and Bhabani Bhattacharya, and such playwrights as Karnad, Rakesh, Sircar, and Tendulkar deal with the theme of social deformity and its evil impact on human life.

Manchi Sarat Babu rightly remarks:

> Tendulkar successfully brings out the ugly cultural deformity of our society through his plays. He depicts gender deformity in *Kamala*, political deformity in *Ghashiram Kotwal,* physical deformity in *Sakharam Binder*, mental deformity in *Encounter in Umbugland* and *Kanyadan*, and spiritual deformity in *The Vultures*.[5]

Manchi Sarat Babu further observes: "He (Tendulkar) does not touch upon social deformity exclusively in any of his plays."[6] However, one feels that it is present in all his plays, although it is not elaborately dealt with in this or that play.

Tendulkar's plays dwell on the existing reality of human life with all its limitations. The subject-matter of his plays is mostly related to man, his conscience, his ego, his body, his association, etc. They focus on disharmony between man and society, that is, individual identity and social existence. They project, without any restrictions or reservations, the filth and the squalor he has noticed around in the society of his day.

In Tendulkar's plays, a type of class-consciousness is noticeable. In most of his plays, he attacks white-collar middle-class values and moral code. The plays deal with conflict and confrontation between an individual and the society. The theatre group in the play *Silence! The Court is in Session* as referred to earlier represents "a miniscule cross-section of middle-class society."[7] While depicting the problem of unmarried motherhood, Tendulkar exposes the double standards of the cultured, educated people, along with their sadist tendencies and hidden sense of failure. Miss Benare is cunningly made the scapegoat by her companions who consider themselves upholders of the moral values of society. She is punished for the offence she has not committed. None of her companions feels sorry for her for she is leading a solitary life in the "man-centred"[8] world. Through the life story of Miss Benare, the playwright seems to suggests that the crime of hunting innocent people will be repeated as long as this "man-centred" world does not become "human-centred" one.

The play *A Friend's Story* depicts the society which gets a sadistic pleasure in inflicting miseries on a deformed girl Mitra. She is punished severely for having an affair with Nama, but Dalvi goes unnoticed despite the fact he openly ditches one girl after another.

The play *The Vultures* represents such people, who are the victims of cultural degradation in the so-called civilized society. Education fails to remove the barbaric, selfish, sensual, violent, wicked, and sadistic tendencies in their minds. Tendulkar successfully portrays these baser aspects of human nature through their actions and their language. The tragedy of Rama and Rajaninath brings out the irony of human life that the virtuous people suffer for no fault of theirs.

The plays *Silence! The Court is in Session* and *The Vultures* deal with the violence of the educated people in cultured middle-class society while the play *Sakharam Binder* deals with the violence of an uneducated protagonist from a lower stratum of society. Sakharam, a book-binder, does not believe in the institution of marriage and enters into a contractual agreement with a woman in all her helplessness. Laxmi is the seventh one in the series of "his women." The play explores complexities of human nature through delineation of Sakharam's relationship with the two women, Laxmi and Champa. The character of Sakharam symbolizes those people who pretend to help others but are actually the source of the very evil in society. The inhuman sufferings, both physical and mental, that he inflicts upon his women, indicate the violence that exists in the minds of male members of society. The restrictions that he imposes on his women reflect a man's inherent inclination to dominate a woman.

Another important aspect of the play is woman-woman relationship. Laxmi is portrayed as sensitive, hardworking, and religious while Champa is portrayed as rebellious, gross, and sensual. However, Laxmi turns out to be vicious and incites Sakharam to kill Champa, for she is her rival in love. Champa, on the other hand, shows great generosity towards Laxmi by giving her shelter even in the teeth of Sakharam's opposition. However, there is "a touch of contempt in Champa's treatment of Laxmi, the contempt that a stronger person feels for a weakling."[9]

Tendulkar's plays represent women as a class. They have a unique role to play in the plays' action. The women characters portrayed are of two types: (i) sensitive, tender-hearted, and generous and (ii) rebellious, dominant, and assertive. Benare, Rama, Sarita, and Jyoti represent intellectually crippled generation of women who are conscious of the injustice imposed on them, but they neither bear any will nor show any guts to rebel against their male-counterparts. Therefore, they themselves are responsible for their miseries and sufferings to a large extent. The character of Sarita in the play *Kamala* exemplifies that the so-called education has provided just sophisticated and refined slaves instead of the earlier unsophisticated and barbaric ones to their male-counterparts.

The character of Vijaya, in the play *Encounter in Umbugland,* differs from other women characters in Tendulkar's plays. Through her, Tendulkar has successfully portrayed, like Ibsen's Nora or Shaw's Candida, a "New Woman" who is courageous, emotionally restrained, morally strong, clever, clear-headed, and determined. She is also one of those women of contemporary Indian culture who have initiated new conventions and new traditions. That is why she successfully turns the tables on her advisers and triumphantly carries out her well-devised plans of vanquishing her enemies.

Kamala and Gauri, are such innocent women as are not even conscious of the injustice inflicted on them. Therefore, they cannot help themselves but are victimized by the ambitions and achievements of their male counterparts.

Thus, Tendulkar's plays deal with social deformity in its varied aspects and brings out its evil consequences on human life in terms of mind-set, sex, and class.

Basically, society has always been divided into two classes. In the ancient classical period, there were masters and slaves; in the medieval age, they were transformed into landlords and serfs or tenants. Ever since the industrial revolution, society has been divided into two classes, capitalists and labourers. In our usual parlance, we address them as the haves and the have-nots. The division is economical one, where the upper-class people suffer from superiority complex and the lower-class people from inferiority complex. The power game played by these people to win over their acquired complexes is the real cause of political deformity.

The power game comprises three major roles: (i) the Persecutor, (ii) the Victim, and (iii) the Rescuer. Role shifting is a common phenomenon at individual level. These three roles according to Karpman form a " Drama Triangle",[10] which is a characteristic feature not only of a play or a story, but of human life also. Steiner calls this triangle—"a Rescue Triangle."[11] The play *Ghashiram Kotwal* best illustrate the concept of Drama Triangle.

The setting of the play *Ghashiram Kotwal* takes us back to the period of the 18th century Indian history, that of the Peshwa regime in Maharashtra. However, it may be seen as Tendulkar's dramatic comment on power politics in society, as the ideas put forward here are common to all ages and societies. An unknown

Marathi critic writing in a very reputed literary journal discusses *Ghashiram Kotwal* thus:

> The myth in the play gives the evidence of Tendulkar's extraordinary imagination. Using the classical and the folk elements such as Dashavatara, Gaulan, Tamasha, etc., he creates a suitable form according to the demands of the situations.[12]

But there are two very serious charges levelled against the play and the playwright: (i) The play has been highly criticized as being anti-Brahmin, and (ii) Tendulkar is accused of distorting history. Tendulkar's reply to this criticism is as stated below:

> This is not a historical play. Although based on historical legend, I have no intention of commentary on the morals, or lack of them, of the Peshwa, of Nana Phadnavis or Ghashiram. The moral of the story, if there is any, may be looked for elsewhere.[13]

According to Girish Karnad, in *Ghashiram Kotwal,* Tendulkar deals with the theme of "emergence of demons in public", created by political leaders for the fulfilment of their aims.[14]

Ghashiram, a poor Brahmin from Kanauj, leaves the city of Poona as being tortured and humiliated on the false charge of theft. The inhuman treatment transforms an innocent newcomer into an ambitious, sadistic perpetrator who does not hesitate to bargain his daughter's chastity to Nana for a pecuniary gain of being the Kotwal of the city of Poona. Nana is seen actually exercising his power through Ghashiram, the Kotwal. However, Ghashiram is too full of revenge against the Brahmins of Poona. For the time being, he is not aware of the treacherous ways of Nana. The city of Poona starts trembling at the mention of his name due to his tyrannical rule, restrictions and punishments. Gauri's death at the hands of a midwife during abortion of the babe she has conceived by Nana makes him more ruthless and sadistic. Twenty-one people who are caught red-handed in the act of stealing fruits from Ghashiram's garden die of suffocation in the unventilated cellar. This genocide becomes the cause of Ghashiram's downfall. Nana does not shield him. He is handed over to the angry Brahmins who stone him to death. Thus, Ghashiram's role constantly changes from Victim to Rescuer (because he provides a kind of relief to Nana by sending his daughter to him), from Rescuer to Persecutor, and finally from Persecutor to Victim. Such a kind of transformation, which may be seen also as role shifting, is noticeable in the roles played by the Brahmins of Poona and Nana, too.

The Brahmins, who torture Ghashiram at the beginning, perform the role of Persecutor. They become the Victims of Ghashiram's anger and frustration, after he becomes the Kotwal of the city. Towards the end of the play, they are shown returning to their previous role of Persecutors, when they punish Ghashiram for his indiscriminate, heartless cruelty.

Another role that is observed in the play is that of a Stage-Manager. It is performed by Nana. Ghashiram's ambition gives him a chance to work out his desire successfully. He seeks erotic pleasure with Gauri and exercise his power through Ghashiram. Gauri's ignominious death makes him conscious of the fact that Ghashiram may prove harmful to him also. So, he offers him to the bloodthirsty mob, that can avenge the wrongs done to them by Ghashiram.

Thus, from the beginning of the play to its end, Nana manages and at times manipulates to bring about changes in the role of Ghashiram and in that of the Brahmins according to the necessity of circumstance. He performs the role of Rescuer twice; for Ghashiram, when he appoints him as the Kotwal, and the other time for the people, when he hands Ghashiram over to the frenzied mob.

> Oswald Summerton, an Australian Transactional Analyst adds two more roles, the Spectator and the Stage-Manager, to the three roles of the Drama Triangle. While Peshwa remains the Spectator, Nana becomes the Stage-Manager, managing the power game in which Ghashiram, who persecutes the people of Poona ruthlessly, finally ends up as their Victim by being mercilessly humiliated and murdered by them.[15]

The play *Sakharam Binder* and *Kanyadan* exemplify the power struggle at family level. The shifting of roles implicit in the Drama Triangle is noticeable in both these plays also.

Sakharam, the play's protagonist leaves the house at the age of eleven due to the barbaric treatment of his father to him. Though he is born in a Brahmin family, he lives like "a Mahar, a dirty scavenger" (127) to show off his arrogance and powerlessness. His exceptional mode of behaviour is a kind of revenge sought on the Brahminical tradition he hates, like Narayanappa's in Anant Moorthy's brilliant novella *Samskara*.

Sakharam does not believe in the institution of marriage. He gives shelter to the needy and helpless women. The woman has to provide him physical enjoyment and domestic comfort. Laxmi, the seventh one in the series of his women, succeeds in re-Brahminizing Sakharam. However, in his association with Champa later, he is transformed into a sensual drunkard. Laxmi's arrival for the second time creates a psychological turmoil in Sakharam, which leaves him impotent. Champa gives shelter to Laxmi but there is a streak of contempt in her treatment to the latter. The kind, tender-hearted Laxmi cannot bear to see Champa as her rival in love. As a result, she uses the policy of "using a thorn to take out a thorn" (63) like Nana does in *Ghashiram Kotwal*. She informs Sakharam of Champa's illicit relationship with Daud Miyan. Sakharam cannot bear this and strangles Champa to death.

Thus, Sakharam's role shifts from Victim to Rescuer, from Rescuer to Persecutor and Laxmi's from Victim to Persecutor. Similarly, Champa's role shifts from Victim to Rescuer and from Rescuer to Victim.

In the play *Kanyadan*, Nath and his daughter Jyoti play the role of Rescuers for Arun by lifting him up out of the mire of orthodoxy and casteism, but both of them become his Victims later in the play, the one just mentally but the other both mentally and physically.

Tendulkar's three plays *Ghashiram Kotwal, Sakharam Binder*, and *Kanyadan*, thus, illustrate how the characters' roles change according to the necessity of circumstance. The discussion can be summarized in the axiomatic statement made by one critic: "Yesterday's Victim is today's Victimizer."[16] Thus, it can be concluded that power or lack of power that manifests itself in political deformity is a characteristic aspect of Tendulkar's major plays.

Norman O. Brown, a psychologist,[17] sees in primitive man a perfect harmony between mind and body. However, in the process of civilization, mind and body are divided and alienated from each other, and the ultimate result is physical deformity. Gender deformity and social deformity, at times, cause physical deformity. Gender deformity divides human beings into men and women and social deformity, into manual labourers and intellectuals. These divisions indirectly throw light on physical deformity also.

In his naturalistic play *Sakharam Binder,* Tendulkar projects the crude perversion of individuals, caused by physical deformity. The play moves around the triangular relationship of Laxmi-Sakharam-Champa. Each of them is abnormal in his or her own way. However, they are the victims of circumstances and not of any inherent wickedness.

> The world portrayed in the play *Sakharam Binder* is obscene, physical, and sexual. The people in this world reveal their innermost thoughts in the rustic language they speak. It tends to destroy subtle sensibility. This world is not completely alien to the audience. It disturbs them, however, by shocking their moral consciousness.[18]

Sakharam's cruelty arises from a greater misery. The violent constant beating of his Brahmin father makes him leave the house at the age of eleven. Born of a Brahmin father and a Mahar mother, Sakharam introduces himself: "I'm a Mahar, a dirty scavenger" (127). It indirectly suggests the kind of family background he has as inheritance. The bitter experiences in childhood make him grow like a desert cactus. To smoke tobacco, to drink liquor, and to indulge in sheer mechanical sex are the means that he has adopted to overcome his feeling of frustration.

Sakharam remains unmarried throughout his life as he does not believe in the institution of marriage. So, he arranges a kind of informal husband-and-wife relationship without marriage in his house by giving shelter to a woman in all helplessness. However, the woman suffers a constant humiliation and severe beating at his instance. Although Sakharam is seen criticizing his father for his brutality, he himself metes out brutal treatment to his women.

Laxmi's relationship with Sakharam brings about some good changes in the latter's stormy life, but the relationship does not last for a long time. Due to the sharp contrast in their nature, they cannot satisfy each other either physically or mentally. Laxmi's refusal to allow Daud in joining the prayer of Lord Ganesha and Sakharam's violent beating to Laxmi in its aftermath become the cause of their separation.

After Laxmi, Sakharam brings Champa. The younger, better built, slightly more plump, and a lot sensual Champa transforms the religious-minded, responsible householder Sakharam into a sensual drunkard.

Laxmi's separation from Sakharam proves temporary, as she returns to him fascinated within a few months. Champa pities her and gives her shelter against Sakharam's stern objection. However,

> the presence of Laxmi and Champa at the same time has a strange effect on Sakharam. It is as if the two different strands in his character come into direct confrontation, creating a psychological turmoil in him and resulting in his temporary impotence.[19]

Champa's illicit relationship with Daud, his friend, turns Sakharam mad with anger. In consequence, he strangles her to death. Towards the end of the play, he gets an emotional support from Laxmi, who helps him cover up the murder and get rid of the feeling of remorse. "Anyway she was a sinner. She'll go to hell. Not you. I've been a virtuous woman. My virtuous deeds will see both of us through" (196).

Thus, each character in the play is the combination of strength and weakness. Outwardly, Laxmi appears kind and generous, but she exhibits her viciousness in her treacherous behaviour towards Champa. She frankly develops a friendship with Fauzdar Shinde, Champa's husband and finds nothing wrong about it. But her moral sense is outraged by Champa's sexual relationship with Daud. There is a definite development in her character from a simple, generous, sensitive woman into a cunning, ruthless, determined lady who devises the plan of defeating her rival and carries out her decision successfully.

Champa is apparently gross and violent. However, she shows strange kindness while giving shelter to Laxmi who returns in all helplessness. No doubt, she is aggressive, but her violence is not without any reasons. Her mother's total disregard for her and also her husband's inhuman treatment to her make her coarse and violent. She appears human throughout the play. So, "she does not suffer from powerlessness as Sakharam and Laxmi do."[20]

The play Sakharam Binder deals with the complexity in human nature. It treats varied aspects of sex and violence. According to Tendulkar,

> Even in the plays like *Sakharam Binder* and *The Vultures*, the theme is not violence. Violence comes as a way of life—a natural way of life, if you consider the background of the characters. It is there as a part of functioning of a character.[21]

Violence is an inevitable aspect of their lives, nature, and culture. Therefore, Manchi Sarat Babu is quite justified in stating: "The inhuman violence of the human characters in these plays is only the result of the physical deformity."[22] Violence characterizes the play, because it is inherent to the very lifestyles of the characters.

The protagonist of the play *A Friend's Story* Mitra suffers from physical deformity. She is a lesbian. Although she tries hard, she cannot get over the deformity. All the efforts of her family members such as fixing her marriage, providing her opportunities having a close intimacy with her proposed life partner, etc., come to noting. However, she feels neither thrilled by his touch nor attracted towards him. Likewise, she neither feels awkward nor fights shy in the company of boys.

The sexual experiment with her servant leaves her to feel that she is far from being a man's wife. However, looking at her, one cannot guess about her 'abnormality.' She has a charming personality that fascinates the college-boys towards her. Pande, for example, likes her and falls in love with her. He leaves the city and joins the army, however, when he realizes that Mitra, a homo, cannot become his beloved.

Nama's close, intimate association renders Mitra conscious of her own sensuality. She cannot bear Nama in the company of Dalvi, her boyfriend. Even Nama's jocular statement that she is getting married, renders her wild and ferocious. She finds it difficult to restrain herself. But Nama moves away from her and ceases to have any more interest in her. Estrangement from Nama and Bapu leaves her life miserable and meaningless. She tries to be feminine but fails in the attempt. Frustrated as she is, she commits suicide. To quote it in the words of Rohini Hattangady: "The playwright tries to understand Mitra through Bapu. As Bapu fails, so do we! The end is inevitable."[23]

Fragmented mind is a gift of modern, civilized society. Originally, each individual has the capacity to understand the world. However, society is divided on the basis of caste, class, colour, religion, sex, etc. These divisions distort the primal unity between mind and body. Hogie Wyckoff, a Transactional Analyst, observes: "Men are encouraged to develop their rationality and to suppress their intuition while women are encouraged to develop their intuition and to suppress their rationality."[24]

These basic classes are themselves divided. Educated people or intellectuals are given the official jobs that demand rationality while workers are given manual jobs that demand physical work. This inequality in the works invades human mind and makes him/her mentally deformed.

The play *Encounter in Umbugland* exposes the evils in the political field. It shows how politicians make the people mindless by suppressing their capacity to think and by arousing their emotions.

Actually, the play reflects the political scene of India in the late sixties and early seventies. The question: "After Nehru, Who?" finds an echo in the play "After Vichitravirya, Who?" (284).

The story represents then the political situation of India and the characters represent the historical personages. No doubt, the playwright successfully tries to keep a distance, but one can easily identify the characters with the political figures of the day who held ministerial positions in those years. The most important character in the play is that of Vijaya. The play exhibits her development from a headstrong, politically inexperienced princess into an intelligent, witty ruler.

After Vichitravirya's death, each minister tries to occupy the throne, but none becomes successful due to the lack of unity. So, they unanimously decide to make Vijaya their queen and to rule the country in her name. Vijaya, at first, rejects the responsibility, as she wants to have her freedom. However, Prannarayan helps her accept the responsibility and guides her in her journey from a Princess to a ruler. In the course of time, she learns to enjoy power by suppressing her humanity. That is why she remains victorious over her rivals.

It is through the character of Prannarayan and through the device of the masked men that Tendulkar throws light on the ugliness and futility of power game. From Prannarayan's guidance to Princess Vijaya, the audience becomes aware of the fact that conspiracy and treachery are the characteristic features of the present-day politics. Deceitfulness is the way of life in it. Victory is impossible without resorting to treacherous ways and means. As quoted earlier, "A show of sacrifice is always profitable in politics" (306). A ruler should always remind himself that each of the persons is more important than the next. One should not be true to oneself and play false to others in politics. To accept and to digest these unpalatable things is difficult for a common and truthful person. So, the ruler does not need to be human, he should be either superhuman or dehumanized. Vijaya's development from a Princess to a successful ruler bears evidence to the above-mentioned facts of power politics.

The play projects how falsehood has become an inevitable part of the politician's life, the ultimate result of which is hypocritical behaviour. In order to enjoy power, the politicians "allow themselves to be dehumanized."[25] The play consists of a critique not only on the rulers but on the ruled also. Both of them are mentally deformed. The rulers go on deceiving their subjects and the subjects blindly trust their leaders. The play ends with Prannarayan criticising people in the words: "I see you upside down, a formless, characterless, lifeless, existenceless gathering. The blind, deaf, and dumb spectators of the whole encounter—who allow men to become politicians, politicians to become statesmen, statesmen to become cunning men, and cunning men to become robots, mechanical men" (356).

The play *Kanyadan* depicts mental deformity of a daughter while she is pursuing the ideals of her father. Nath Devalalikar and Seva, the parents of Jyoti and Jaiprakash, are social activists. They try their best to eradicate the social evil of untouchability in society. So, Nath is all praise for his daughter's decision to marry a Dalit poet. Due to the encouragement of her father, Jyoti ignores her mother's warning about her proposed love-marriage and the married life afterwards. All the efforts of her mother to convince her that it will be impossible for her to cope with the situation after marriage as she has been nurtured in middle-class sophisticated culture, prove in vain. Father supports Jyoti and she marries Arun.

However, their marriage, instead of being a source of happiness, proves a nightmare. Seva's fears and anxieties come true. Arun's consciousness of Jyoti's upper-class origin makes him feel inferior and restless. To get rid of his inferiority complex and to show his manliness, he gets drunk and beats Jyoti inhumanly despite her pregnancy. Jyoti returns to her parents seeking shelter and protection but her father makes her go with Arun, and asks her not to care for her personal happiness but to save the intercaste marriage which is, in his view, "a wonderful experiment" (537) in itself.

Arun's autobiography gets him an acclaim as a writer in society. But good social status does not bring any change in the brutal treatment he metes out to his wife. Nath cannot bear his dual personality. Still he praises Arun in his speech thinking that his refusal to give a felicitation speech in his honour may cause more troubles to Jyoti. However, Jyoti likes neither her father's insincere speech nor his justification of the same. The play ends with the charge that her father has rendered her mentally crippled by his false, hollow idealism. "Someone said these people kidnap little children, break their limbs and make them crippled. Bhai, forgive me for my words, but you have made us..." (566).

Nath becomes more pathetic than Seva as he compels Jyoti to go with Arun. That is why he confesses: "You warned me several times. But I didn't pay any attention I had this maniacal urge to uproot casteism and caste distinctions from our society. As a result, I pushed my own daughter into the sea of misery..." (557).

Nath's faith in his ideals renders him blind. He believes that the Dalits are aware of what suffering is. To acquire a place and position as human beings, they have endured a lot of suffering. So, the Dalits, who have undergone so much of suffering, should not put others to torture. However, his son Jaiprakash gives him a kind of revelation that the victims of wickedness and violence derive a sadistic pleasure in perpetrating the same brutal violence on others. That is why the hope that experience of pain and misery enables man to acquire dignity or nobility is false and vain. On the contrary, "...he can only become a greater devil", since "yesterday's victim 'becomes' today's victimizer" (547).

The main cause of the suffering of Jyoti and Arun is their mental deformity, the inferiority complex of Arun and Jyoti's frustrated, if not futile, efforts to translate her father's ideals into reality. Nath and Jyoti become mindless in playing the progressive role of reformers and Arun becomes mindless in his effort to overcome his awareness of low-class origin. Thus, it may be inferred that the play treats of mindlessness. It is seen operating at two levels, idealistic and sentimental. The former is perceived in the father-and-daughter relationship and the latter in the husband-and-wife relationship.

The play *A Friend's Story* slightly hints at the theme of mental deformity. It is perceptible in the characters of Nama and Dalvi. Nama is involved with Mitra as well as Dalvi, just physically and not emotionally. When she is in the company of Mitra, it seems that a man called Dalvi did not exist for her. Surprisingly enough, when Dalvi asks her to leave Mitra's room, she behaves in an indifferent manner. Observing Nama's double game, Bapu becomes restless and says: "The funny thing was, Nama was hardly seen with Dalvi, and when she was with him, she pretended not to see me. This double dealing must have been difficult. And yet people indulge in it. Why? Why couldn't Nama take a decision once and for all?" (460).

Nama is being dual with Bapu also. In the absence of Mitra, she complains to Bapu about her, while in her presence, she joins her in her attempt to tease him. At last, she remains neither with Mitra nor with her boy friend Dalvi. Instead, she goes to Calcutta and gets married.

Manya Dalvi is a kind of "mavalli" or rogue. Ditching girls is a usual affair with him. He blackmails Nama like several other girls before. Paradoxically enough, when Mitra goes his way, he punishes her severely by ruining all her future prospects. So as referred to above, it seems that there is something odd about the nature of the two, Nama and Dalvi. It is their mental deformity which does not allow them to persist with their relationship.

Human civilization has witnessed all through its history a kind of schism between body and soul, leading to spiritual malady and disease. Quest for power and position renders people blind and cripples their souls. This leads to spiritual deformity, which manifests itself in human violence and destructiveness.

Most of Tendulkar's plays deal with the themes related to love, sex, and violence. They have become rather noticeable in some glaring light ever since the presentation of *The Vultures*. The play projects violence in human nature through the depiction of an upper middle-class family. Hari Pitale, the father of the two sons Ramakant and Umakant and a daughter

Manik, prospers in his business by cheating his brother. The two sons and the daughter inherit his treacherous ways. Ultimately, "they form a family of vultures."[26]

Not satisfied with the magnitude of their father's property, Ramakant and Umakant decide to blackmail the Raja of Hondur, their sister's lover. However, they cannot carry out their plan due to the Raja's death. In anger and frustration, they cause abortion of their sister's babe.

Constant drinking of liquor affects Ramakant's health adversely and he grows impotent. So, his wife Rama turns to Rajaninath, the illegitimate son of Hari Pitale for emotional support. The relationship results into her wilful conception or pregnancy. Anyhow, she gets her urge for motherhood fulfilled. However, Manik seeks her revenge on her brothers by manoeuvring Rama's abortion.

Feeling insecure, Hari Pitale turns to Rajaninath for protection. Father tells the illegitimate son that he has a mind to change his will, but Rajaninath has no attraction for any worldly possessions. It is these material considerations that turn the Pitales into loveless vultures. Without showing compassion, he asks his father to leave his garage.

The play is realistic not only in the portrayal of characters and their actions but in the language and setting also. The playwright, here, depicts educated, modern generation. But the language used by them is full of abusive terms such as bastard, swine, lecher, etc. All the actions take place in a dim light quite away from the outer world of cultured, refined people. Due to the presence of this dim light, the play appears to present a detective story. The picture of a huge tree having curved, crooked, bare branches, and a big hollow, in the background symbolizes the living place of the characters is not a home but a hollow of wild vultures as "home is built by hearts." The dark green shade cast on Rama's *tulsi vrindavan* indicates how the virtuous suffer in the company of vulture-like people. A fierce wind, and a shrill screeching of vultures incline the audience to perceive the play as being full of violence and sensation. Even the name of the family, viz., "Pitale", suggests that the family members are rather brazen, shameless, and insolent.

However, Tendulkar projects something more than wickedness and sensuality. If the world of Ramakant, Umakant, Manik, and Papa represents evil aspects inherent in human nature, the world of Rama and Rajaninath represents its tender aspects. Although Rama's relationship with Rajaninath is illicit one, one should not ignore the fact that it is the only human and genuine one. The poems of Rajaninath help one realize the past history and the present state of the Pitales. Similarly, they indirectly express the playwright's compassion for the victims of viciousness.

Tendulkar succeeds here in depicting the tragedy of Rama and Rajaninath in naturalistic terms. Similarly, by pitting these two worlds of tenderness and violence against each other, he sets a new trend of avant-garde movement—the "Theatre of Cruelty" in Marathi.

Manchi Sarat Babu rightly observes:

> The spiritual deformity facilitates ruthless exploitation and oppression and destroys human relations even within the family.[27]

To conclude the discussion, it can be stated that Tendulkar, like the post-war British, American, playwrights such as Osborne, Tennessee Williams, etc., have written plays dealing with real situations. He has rebelled against the conventional theatre not only in respect of theme and subject-matter but also in that of manner and style. It is for this reason that he is considered iconoclast, i.e., image-breaker bringing people face to face with the realities of their lives. The new drama does not dwell on conventional, stereotyped characterization, viz., actions and reactions of a hero and a villain, and sufferings of a simple, innocent heroine. It has a dominant or central character, i.e., a protagonist, who represents anger and frustration of the post-war generation.

The play *The Vultures,* by and large, treats the victims of cultural degradation. It also depicts the suffering of innocent people, e.g., Rama and Rajaninath, who are leading a life among savages, i.e., Papa, his two sons, and a daughter with the covetousness of vultures. The play *Kamala* projects the story of the success-oriented, civilized contemporary society where the youths are ready to sacrifice human values to pursue their material goals unquestionably. The play *Ghashiram Kotwal* is Tendulkar's comment on power politics in society taking us beyond time and place, despite the fact that the story is based on a historical incident of the 18th century Peshwa regime. The play explores the violence of those people who are created, nurtured, and ruthlessly crushed by political leaders. The play *Kanyadan* deals with anger and commitment of the educated, lower middle-class, young generation with whom violence becomes a day-to-day, routine affair.

Most of the characters in these plays are seen as defeated or frustrated since they acquire deformed personalities. Thus, they seem to have a tragic dimension. Deformity of one sort or another such as gender, social, political, physical, mental, and spiritual is perceptible in Tendulkar's characterization. He seeks to project men and women, not in their brighter, but in their darker aspects. Mostly, they are shown life-like, i.e., as what they are but, at times, they are shown worse than what they are in actuality, particularly in a play like *The Vultures*.

Language, stage directions, setting, costumes, lighting, etc., are in harmony with the play's thematic background. Such plays as *Kanyadan*, *The Vultures, Sakharam Binder*, etc., explore violence at physical, psychological, and verbal levels. The first two are manifest in actions and thoughts of the characters, and the last one, that is, violence at the verbal level finds its best expression in the language, which is too full of abusive, obscene terms and tabooed words. Effective handling of themes and successful delineation of characters realized through setting, costumes, and light and sound effects render the plays' violence vivid, sensational, and impressive. To say it in one word, they breathe "realism."

NOTES

1. G.P. Deshpande, "Shantata! Court Chalu Ahe: Kahi Vichar", *Satyakatha*, 1971, 24. The extract is translated into English by the investigator herself.
2. Kavita Nagpal, "The Badal Sircar Magic", *The Hindustan Times*, 5 April 1992, 13. Manchi Sarat Babu, *Indian Drama Today*, New Delhi: Prestige Books, 1997, 11-12.

3. Simone de Beauvoir, *The Second Sex*, New York: Vintage, 1989.
4. Arundhati Banerjee, Introduction, *Five Plays of Vijay Tendulkar,* Bombay: OUP, 1992, xvii.
5. Manchi Sarat Babu, *Indian Drama Today,* New Delhi: Prestige Books, 1997, 51.
6. *Ibid.*
7. Arundhati Banerjee, Introduction, *Five Plays of Vijay Tendulkar,* Bombay: OUP, 1992, viii.
8. J.M. Waghmare, "Literature of Marginality", in N.M. Aston (ed.), *Literature of Marginality: Dalit Literature and African-American Literature,* New Delhi: Prestige Books, 2001, 24.
9. Arundhati Banerjee, Introduction, *Five Plays of Vijay Tendulkar,* Bombay: OUP, 1992, xv.
10. Manchi Sarat Babu, *Indian Drama Today,* New Delhi: Prestige Books, 1997, 63.
11. *Ibid.*
12. *Alochana*, May, 1973, 24. The extract is translated into English by the investigator herself.
13. Quoted by Samik Bandyopadhyay, Introduction in Vijay Tendulkar, *Ghashiram Kotwal*, trans. Jayant Karve and Eleanor Zelliot, Calcutta: Seagull Books, 1989, 2.
14. Manchi Sarat Babu, *Indian Drama Today,* New Delhi: Prestige Books, 1997, 72.
15. *Transactional Game Analysis* (Delhi: Manohar, 1979), 153. Quoted in Manchi Sarat Babu, *Indian Drama Today,* New Delhi: Prestige Books, 1997, 75.
16. Vijay Tendulkar, *Kanyadan*, trans., Gauri Ramnarayan, Delhi: OUP, 1996, 51. Quoted in Manchi Sarat Babu, *Indian Drama Today,* New Delhi: Prestige Books, 1997, 79.
17. *Life against Death:* "Appollo and Dionysus", London: Routledge, 1959, 155-76. Quoted in Manchi Sarat Babu, *Indian Drama Today,* New Delhi: Prestige Books, 1997, 83.
18. "Vadagrasta Tharalele Natak *Sakharam Binder:* Vijay Tendulkar", *Alochana*, 18-19. The extract by an unknown critic is a translation by the investigator herself.
19. Arundhati Banerjee, Introduction, *Five Plays of Vijay Tendulkar,* Bombay: OUP, 1992, xiv-xv.
20. Manchi Sarat Babu, *Indian Drama Today*, New Delhi: Prestige Books, 1997, 93.
21. Vijay Tendulkar, "Interview", *The Indian Express,* March 27, 1983, Magazine Sections, quoted in Manchi Sarat Babu, *Indian Drama Today,* New Delhi: Prestige Books, 1997, 93.

22. Manchi Sarat Babu, *Indian Drama Today*, New Delhi: Prestige Books, 1997, 93.
23. Rohini Hattangady, Appendix III "Note on *A Friend's Story*" *Collected Plays in Translation,* New Delhi: OUP, 2003, 595.
24. Hogie Wyckoff, "Sex Role Scripting in Men and Women", Claude M. Steiner (ed.), *Scrpits People Live* (New York: Bantam, 1980), 196-209. Quoted in Manchi Sarat Babu, *Indian Drama Today,* New Delhi: Prestige Books, 1997, 100.
25. Manchi Sarat Babu, *Indian Drama Today*, New Delhi: Prestige Books, 1997, 115.
26. *Ibid.*, 139.
27. *Ibid.*, 150.

APPENDIX

FACE-TO-FACE WITH VIJAY TENDULKAR

—Shailaja Wadikar
—L.S. Deshpande

[Having a word with a living writer is a thrilling experience.] To meet Vijay Tendulkar has been my day-night dream. The dream becomes a reality on 13th March, 2007. The visit was a pleasant experience because of the company and help given by my well-wisher Anand Deshpande. We (Dr. L.S. Deshpande, my Guru, and myself) had the golden opportunity of spending an afternoon with the veteran dramatist of India. The moment we entered the room, we saw the following lines inscribed on the door-glass of the almirah:

God, grant me serenity
to accept the things
I cannot change,
courage to change the things
I can,
and wisdom
to know the difference.

I was greatly impressed by his dynamic personality. The determination and serenity on his face left me spell-bound. His vision, I felt, was an index to his greatness. After having a dialogue with him, I felt, what Lewis Carroll said, apts Tendulkar very well.

You may charge me with murder—
Or want of sense
(we are all of us weak at times):

But the slightest approach to a false pretence
Was never among my crimes!

[Here, I'm sharing my joy with you.]

Q.1 Are your plays really problem plays, Sir? If they are so, can they be compared with Ibsen's or Shakespeare's plays?

Ans. I don't have any opinion on that. I write, whatever strikes me. What opinion can be there? The truth is the play does not emerge from air. Whatever is there in my life, or people's lives, is reflected in my plays. There is very little fictitious in my plays. Wherever there is man, there are problems. I haven't written plays to present the problems. I didn't intend to take up a problem nor was I bent on solving any. That was never a part of my writing process. Wherever there was any problem in my play, it served as a background. But I've no solution to offer. Whether to call them problem plays is a big question. It's like designating contemporary plays as tragedies in the Greek sense of the word. However, I'm least interested in calling my plays problem plays. There is no problem there; there are human-situations instead. The characters in the plays find themselves entangled in the grip of their situations. I've never written my plays, exclusively, to treat the problems.

Q.2 Have you written plays to change the mindset of people?

Ans. No. Never so. In one sense, you'll find therein my own expression of the moment. They are all reflections of my mind.

Q.3 Would you call yourself an iconoclast?

Ans. My plays depicted my concerns, my tensions, my joys. Whether people liked to see them or not was not my question. I had drama as a form to handle. So, I wrote the plays. To do something good or bad to society at large was never my intention. Moreover, I have reservations as to whether society changes or not by witnessing plays.

Q.4 Shaw and Ibsen are non-conformists. You, too, are non-conformist. But they are not controversial like you. Your comment, please.

Ans. I've no opinion about that. You might have gathered that impression, perhaps.

Q.5 But do you feel that you are an iconoclast?

Ans. No. I have no mind to be that nor have I planned to be that. I haven't deliberately written plays to do some good or bad to the people. To explore myself, my life, my thoughts and to strive constantly to discover "something" in life—that's the sole intention of my writing.

Q.6 Do you believe like Dada Dharmadhikari that a woman has a right to have a child outside wedlock? Do you believe in the concept of Virgin Mother?

Ans. The same response I'll reiterate. Whatever was there in my mind was reflected in my plays. Whatever occurred in the life around, I got in my plays. We have our own reactions to the situations. Nevertheless, I have written plays with no particular ideology in mind.

Q.7 It seems, your perspective is amoral, non-committal. Complexity and ambiguity characterise your plays. Actually, they constitute the strength of your plays, because they bring in multiple meanings. Comment, please.

Ans. As a dramatist, I always consider myself non-committal. If I am committed, there won't be any option left. I don't like that. Basically, my writing process goes thus: I'm in quest of something; so, I write and not because I've discovered something and it's worth depicting.

Q.8 Do you think that you have projected man smaller than he actually is?

Ans. No, I don't think so. I projected people as I saw them. I don't want to disturb their proportion. I try to seek them, search them (as they are, and not as they look to me). I'm curious about having a close scrutiny of them all. But I've never imposed my personal feelings and thoughts on them. In my quest of their true selves, I notice that they are not complete. True, I'm in quest, and I go wherefrom I can have a better glance of them.

Q.9 Do your plays reveal a progressive, humanist ideology? Freedom, from your point of view, seems to be the greatest value, may be for good or bad. But it is the right of every individual. None can deny that. Do you want to communicate this sense of humanism through your plays?

Ans. I'm the product of my generation, a part of it. During those times, idealism was in the air. Things related to it were also ideal. I was under the influence of those things. However, they were not consciously reflected in my writing. While living, as a man, I take certain positions but once I sit up for writing, I'm objective to the extent possible. I've been exploring how men behaved in their mutual relationship with others.

I can't manage to sit up and think confined to one place. The opinions I give, relate to the actual time when I'm speaking. There is nothing in them beyond. But when I sit up for writing, I write going beyond my personal feelings, emotions, and thoughts. I'm least concerned as to whether it is right or wrong. I always try to project everything very objectively. I go beyond what exists around me. I don't get into the trap of words. However, it doesn't mean that there is no effort on my part. There is always objective depiction to the extent it is possible. Suppose, I am very furious at something. But when I start writing, keeping aside my personal wrath, for the time being, I write easily and spontaneously. I've an urge to understand the subject neatly and properly. I don't allow my personal feelings to interfere with the process. There is something that happens automatically and I just communicate it. And there is no special effort involved. Once I sit up for writing, I don't take any stance. That's an altogether a different state of mind. Thus, the writing happens automatically, I don't need to do anything special.

Q.10 Sir, each of your plays has a message to give. Do you agree?

Ans. If you look for it, you'll see it there. Each play contains several messages. There is no point giving a message, deliberately, however. The thing is that the audience in a certain state of mind derive a message from what they watch. Whatever I reveal, is very genuine and authentic, indeed. I'm not being romantic. Whatever I see, I depict, clearly and uninhibitedly. The audience can obtain several messages from it. But I for one have no message to offer, or anything of the sort. I want to understand man, and the situation in which he is placed, and the time he belongs to. I don't make any demands on my audience or readers. It does happen sometimes, that I set out for one destination but reach another. That's all about it.

Q.11 Do you think it happened with *Kanyadan* that you intended to say one thing but you said something else?

Ans. No. It's not so, in *Kanyadan*. I said whatever I meant. One thing we have to bear in mind that while watching the play, the social issues of the time, social circumstances affect the play adversely. When for the first time, *Kanyadan* was staged, the problem of reservation was on the anvil. There were hot debates among the public. Naturally, something pro-Dalit, anti-Dalit had been already there in the audience's minds. However, I had no such thoughts in my mind. Actually, it is no Dalit play; it doesn't deal with their problem. To speak the truth, Nath is the play's protagonist. So, it is a play of my generation. Virtually, I was trying to find in it what happened to my generation. However, there is a Dalit strain in it and it has come naturally. But to make a comment on the Dalits was not my object, for the Dalit Arun Athawale is a subsidiary character and is not the protagonist as supposed. The protagonist is Nath Devalalikar. And it has come clearly and straightforwardly in the play.

Q.12 Is the conflict of values delineated in your plays?

Ans. The conflict of values is always there. There is nothing new about it. You can call it a conflict, or tension, or anything you like.

Q.13 Call it perversion or sinfulness, it is there in your plays. The dark side of life is prominently projected there. Your comment, please.

Ans. I think, I'm very curious about those people who are "fallen", "defeated", and without any receiving side and are the least societal people. I must understand them. But what you are calling conflict, is not implied there. The tolerance, the tenacity they exhibit is fascinating for me. Benare collapses at last, so does Sakharam. It's all true. Ramakant in *The Vultures* has to suffer impotency. I've love, immense love, for them, who aspire to get something beyond the situation in which they are placed. These are the very people who try to catch life beyond living and get lost in the process. I don't have any feeling for the people, who go dually—they say one thing and do another.

Q.14 The protagonists of your plays such as Sakharam, Ghashiram, etc., sometimes appear to be anti-heroes. Have you intended to project them as such?

Ans. I don't categorise them as heroes, anti-heroes, villains, etc. Even if I am angry with somebody, I don't see him as a villain.

Q.15 Even Narendra Modi also?

Ans. No, no, not at all. Now I'm writing to Narendra Modi expressing my desire to see him. One thing we have to keep in mind is that when we watch man's action from a distance, it has just one dimension. That time, I'll react like any other man. But later on, I grow curious and wish to have a closer view of him. Now, I've met many a time a number of politicians off the record. I want to see what stuff he is made of. I'm angry quite naturally and try to relate him to whatever image I carry of that politician. But apart from that, once I sit up for writing, I won't write anything on Modi in that mood. I want to understand and search him. In my quest of Modi, I've read several books. Among them is Stalin's biography. Seven hundred pages at a stretch I've read, that, too, in minute details. It's based on the latest research. I'm in quest of such individuals—the clay they are made of. It's an endless quest. Finally, I may or may not get it—something I'm in quest of.

Q.16 The women characters, except Vijaya in *Encounter in Umbugland*, seem to be incapable of revolt. Your opinion, please.

Ans. The fact is that majority of the women characters in my plays, except Jyoti in *Kanyadan*, are the representatives of their generations. I see them with my inner eye. Their protest, I feel, goes to the extent, I visualised. It doesn't exceed the limit. However, in one sense, I feel, despite the change in generation, man doesn't seem to be involved in the relationship in the manner, woman is. A man can superficially enter into any relationship and step out of it, but so is not the case of a woman. Even if she is a downright feminist, progressive, conscious, having put up with the relationship for some time, she cannot come out of it like changing clothes. The relationship is life-long and goes deep into the very skin. Many a time, it acts as a hurdle for her. Even now, it is happening, repeatedly. When she has been advised for divorce, when women's groups are formed for demonstration against her husband, (whether in the play or in actual life), who has set her on torture, she is reluctant to act. Why is it so? Because she is still entangled in that relationship. I'm convinced, she cares little for justice or injustice. What we call involvement is quite natural with some individual; and to get out of it is very painful.

Q.17 Sir, most of your plays deal with the theme of love, sex and violence. Do you agree with it?

Ans. You've to do a little more research work for that. You have studied just my translated plays. But if you consider all my plays, you'll see that there are a good number of plays without any violence. In my social observations, I've been watching, besides several other things, violence in its different manifestations. So, there was no cause there to exclude it. I wanted to study and understand what it is and where it comes from, and what these relationships are. I faced all these questions several times. I referred to it in the introduction to the play *Baby*. It happens on occasions that violence becomes the need of both—the one, who tortures and the other who is tortured. That is why there is no breach of relationship there. It's no use to describe it in such broad terms as "sadistic" and "masochistic". They are in a bond of mutual love in several ways. Someone longs someone to torture, and wants be tortured by him or her alone. It's such a wonderful play, indeed! A bond of one sort, a strong bond springs from it.

Q.18 Would you call this sort of violence—psycho-sexual?

Ans. The fact is—categorisation is alien to my nature. In that sense, I'm least academic. Categorise in the way you want. I've nothing to say in that matter. You've your own freedom.

Q.19 Sir, do you think you're a bit cynical?

Ans. No, not in the least. I couldn't project life cynically; absolutely not. That might be my limitation, perhaps. But in my approach to life, I didn't need to have that sort of attitude.

Q.20 The women characters in your plays remind—How difficult it is to dramatise women's lib through situations. Your comment, please.

Ans. Using different words, I'm trying to convince you that women themselves ought to be determined to liberate themselves. There're several modes of liberation. Even though you are a divorcee, you go elsewhere—to a certain town or a country—the involvement continues and never comes to an end. There remains a vacuum and it is very painful for a woman. The difference that one is a man and the other is a woman is superfluous. I think that man and woman are just two elements. The mind is made up of these elements. The extent and the proportion in which we find them determine its structure. It varies from person to person. Some men have a feminine sensibility; surprisingly, some women don't have that. Although the sensibility doesn't seem to be shared; actually, it is shared. That's why I feel that gender discrimination is superfluous.

Q.21 Does the play *Silence! The Court is in Session* depict Benare's individual tragedy or present a horrible picture of societal violence?

Ans. While watching the play *Silence!...*, we come across a complex network of entanglement. The story of Benare's life repeats itself even today. The game, people have started playing is still on. Both the situations are so alike that we won't be able to distinguish them from each other. Whatever is there in our life, can we isolate it from other things? That's why I don't see the things, separately. It's a whole and cannot have separate parts. What I depicted is a human situation. And that human situation is all important and has a variety of manifestations in *Silence!...* What happens to the man in such a situation? Maybe that he's a feeble minded person; he, too, may have to face Benare's predicament. The gender discrimination plays no role here. What counts here is person, or whatever happens to him/her.

Q.22 Does Benare's character give the message: "The too much of innocence is unpardonable in cultured society"?

Ans. Benare's character is not exceptional. However, she is vulnerable. On a thorough going examination of the character, it is noticed that she is frail. Like several others in actuality, she, too, has no real control on her life. The life drags them. Majority of the characters in this play are just like that. Mostly you won't find people in this play who are bent on forging their destinies.

Q.23 Arundhati Banerjee said: "Benare's monologue is reminiscent of Nora's declaration of independence but lacks the note of protest that characterises the speech of Ibsen's heroine." What's your opinion?

Ans. It's her innermost outburst. She doesn't justify herself actually. She hasn't uttered even a single word. It's all there in her mind. So, the entire scene is presented in blue light. We attribute a lot of pride to her. But she hasn't exhibited it in the least.

Q.24 Can the plays *Kamala* and *Ghashiram Kotwal* be designated as topical?

Ans. What will occur to my mind? And wherefrom? There's no rule about that. That's all a part of life. Somehow, life catches me, unawares, and I get it. Some, nay, most of it, eludes me. However, a fraction of it stays with me or haunts me.

I find no need to write the topical. I visualise the situation, I face. *Ghashiram* is not topical to the extent *Kamala* seems to be. Do you really think that *Ghashiram* is topical? I don't have any special interest in history. Although it dwells on a certain historical situation, it is not topical, it is contemporary, in fact. History is not my province. I've intended to stretch the historical situation beyond its confines. I was in the quest of a suitable design. I couldn't get it readily from routine life like in *Kamala* or *Silence!...* There would have been limitations to it. I've made every effort to exceed all those limitations. The play is the evidence.

Q.25 Which value do you think is greater in *Ghashiram Kotwal*—its performance or its literary value?

Ans. The point is—why you distinguish between the two? The play's a play. One can't say that the play's meaning doesn't emerge from its literary value alone. The play has a plot, and is enacted on the stage. What you call performability is the play's real strength. It distinguishes it from other forms of literature. Rather I'm interested in watching a non-literary theatre. It's all good as a theatre. But I least insist on either of them—literary or non-literary. What concerns me is doing justice to the medium, I choose. However, literary value has been an essential constituent of my play. The play's literariness is a source of its strength.

Q.26 How is the theme of love treated in your play *A Friend's Story*—as love's expression or its perversion?

Ans. It's not the play about Mitra's character. It's about her boy-friend, of one who has just entered into her life. He is in such an adolescent state of mind to understand something strange that is happening in his life. It comes to him as a shock. And before he can do anything, it's all over. So, the play actually deals with Mitra's boy-friend rather than Mitra herself. One should relate her to him in the circumstance. The play starts with him and ends with him. It is so simple and straightforward.

Q.27 The characters in the play *The Vultures* are without any streak of goodness? Are there any such individuals in society?

Ans. You've to find it out. I told you that nothing comes out of vacuum. Nowhere, it's suggested that people in society live just like that. Nevertheless, the fact remains. When the men turn vultures, they live like that. They've violence, both spiritual and mental. You may call them spirits, if you like. I've got nothing more to add.

Q.28 Do you think, there is a beast hidden in man rather than an angel?

Ans. I think, the beast is just there. But I prefer the word animal to beast. I like the old word in Marathi *manushyaprani,* i.e. 'human-species.' It signifies the presence of animal in man along with animal instincts. The instincts are all there, permanently. He acts to meet the challenges he poses or the challenges that come his way. Occasionally, he appears to behave like an animal and not like a human. Man has a brain; so, he is expected to behave in a particular fashion. But on many occasions, people seem not to behave like that. So, I feel, they're animals disguised as humans.

Q.29 Man is a victim of deterministic forces. Your comment, please?

Ans. Man surrenders to his fate. All animals are like that. But man alone feels to give a fight against fate. And he'll give a fight. But it is true that there's something like determinism in man's life. But men won't surrender to those forces. Rather they would have an encounter with them. That's why human-species has still survived.

Q.30 Would you call them mere puppets in the hands of fate?

Ans. I'd say: In a sense, they are. But they aren't just puppets. The minor species survive under a circumstance but then they become extinct. I think, man is a little bit greater species. However, it is true that man is subject to fate. Now, there're changes in the bowels of the earth. For example, the tsunami calamity. How can man face it? Despite all the defence mechanism, he discovered and used, the danger persists. Man is feeble and helpless, too. It seems that there have been basic changes in nature. Man has just learnt how to remedy the situation. He's bleak prospects in the years to come. He prides himself that he can do or undo anything, that he will conquer Nature. Now, I feel that pride is lost. It's going. No! it has already gone! But man won't concede his defeat.

Q.31 Do you think that there is anything moral or immoral about love?

Ans. Basically, I think that we should not analyse human actions in terms of good or bad. Does man act in pursuance of the thought of virtue and/or vice? Secondly, I question myself as to who has entitled me, in the capacity of a playwright, to evaluate other's lives. I don't have to lead life like them. So, I can't claim the right to evaluate.

Q.32 Do you feel, Sir, that the characters in your play look more typical than individual?

Ans. No, they are not typical. For me, they're individual. If they aren't so, there won't be any communication link between them and me. If there's no communication, there won't be any dialogue. They must talk and live with me. They'll talk and live under my nose. I won't be able to write unless, I see them face to face, or before my inner eyes, or listen to their dialogues. So, I don't have my characters as types in my mind.

Q.33 Sir, of all the plays, which is your favourite play?

Ans. I don't know it. Whatever I witnessed, I wrote about it.

Q.34 The criticism wrote on your plays....

Ans. I haven't read it. Very rarely, I read about me. I'm least interested in watching documentaries about me. Sometime ago, Amol Palekar organised a festival of my plays in Pune. I didn't go there except on the days of my interviews. So, I can't name my best play. The topic is likely to create confusion. It's better we needn't discuss it.

Q.35 Are there any exotic or native influences on the sources of your plays?

Ans. The fact is—lacking academic discipline, I was rather confused for some time in my reading. I was reading all that was accessible to me. It was no systematic reading, as I had no discipline in the matter. At times, I had my impetus even from newspaper items. For instance, whatever is there in *Kamala*, is based on a news flashed in *India Today*. The core sentence, the play's source goes thus: "He bought me for such and such a sum; how much did he pay for you?"

Q.36 There's a lot of contemporaneity in your plays. Your comment, please.

Ans. Yes, indeed. My plays deal with my times, with the people of my generation.

Q.37 How is it if I describe the plays as realistic?

Ans. But, the word 'realism' has been over-used. My plays contain everything that was there in my personal life, or in people's, or all that I encountered. There is little imaginary or fictitious about it. I've posed no questions irrelevant to my time. Neither was I inclined to write about them nor did I feel about them. In a sense, all this writing of mine is outside the usual dramatic medium; it's wholly personal. For me, there remains something personal about the medium I used. It's all like that. There might

> be some limitations, of course. In short, I don't follow a beaten track; I'm using the genre quite differently.

(At the end of our conversation, I offered the gift, I bought for him. I was about to bend to have his blessings. But he refused both saying: "We're all equals." When I declared, the gift is nothing but a pen, and I bought it as I'm waiting for his next play, he smiled happily. Placing his hand on my head, he blessed me.

I returned home with an overwhelmed heart. The meeting, for me, was a great source of inspiration forever.)

BIBLIOGRAPHY

PRIMARY SOURCES

Tendulkar, Vijay. *Gashiram Kotwal.* Trans. Jayant Karve and Eleanor Zelliot, Calcutta: Seagull Books, 1986.

——. *Kamala, Silence! The Court is in Session, The Vultures, Encounter In Umbugland.* Trans. Priya Adarkar, in *Five Plays of Vijay Tendulkar,* Bombay: OUP, 1992.

——. *Sakharam Binder.* Trans. Kumud Mehta and Shanta Gokhle, in *Five Plays of Vijay Tendulkar,* Bombay: OUP, 1992.

——. *Kanyadan.* Trans. Gouri Ramnarayan, Delhi: OUP, 1996.

——. *Kamala, Silence! The Court is in Session, The Vultures, Encounter In Umbugland.* Trans. Priya Adarkar, *Gashiram Kotwal.* Trans. Jayant Karve and Eleanor Zelliot, *Kanyadan.* Trans. Gouri Ramnarayan, *A Friend's Story* Trans. Gouri Ramnarayan in *Collected Plays in Translation*, New Delhi: OUP, 2002.

SECONDARY SOURCES

Abrams, M.H. *A Glossary of Literary Terms,* Bangalore: Prism, 1993.

Aston, N.M. *Literature of Marginality: Dalit Literature and African-American Literature,* New Delhi: Prestige, 2001.

Bamber, Gascoigne. *Twentieth Century Drama* (London: Hutchson, 1962).

Beautely, Eric, ed. *Second Manifesto: The Theory of the Modern Stage,* Harmondsworth: Penguin, 1983.

Beauvoir, Simone de. *The Second Sex,* New York: Vintage, 1989.

Brooks, Cleanth and Warren, R.P. *Understanding Fiction,* New York: Henry Holt, 1950.

Claude, M. Steiner. *Scripts People Live,* New York: Bantam, 1980.

Dass, Veena Noble. *Modern Indian Drama in English Translation,* New Delhi, 1988.

Deshpande, L.S. *Towards Defining Translatology,* Nanded: Ameya Publishing House, 2001.

Dharan, N.S. *The Plays of Vijay Tendulkar,* New Delhi: Creative, 1999.

Dhawan, R.K., ed. *Indian Literature Today,* 2 Vols. 1, New Delhi: Prestige, 1994.

Esslin, Martin. *Theatre of the Absurd,* London: Penguin, 1968.

Freud, Sigmund. *New Introductory Lectures on Psychoanalysis,* New York: Penguin, 1977.

Fromm, Erich. *The Critics of Psychoanalysis,* London: Jonathan Cape, 1971.

——. *The Anatomy of Human Destructiveness,* New York: Fawcett, 1975.

Ganz, Arthur. *Pinter: A Collection of Critical Essays,* Prentice Hall, 1972.

Gargi, Balwant. *Theatre in India,* New York: Theatre Arts, 1962.

Gaskell, Ronald. *Drama and Reality,* London: Routledge and Kegan Paul, 1972.

George, K.M., ed. *Comparative Indian Literature,* Madras: Macmillan, 1984.

Gowda, Anniah. *Indian Drama,* Mysore: Univ. of Mysore, 1974.

Grene, Nicholas. *Bernard Shaw: A Critical View,* London: Macmillan, 1984.

Hinchliffe, A.P. *The Absurd,* London: Methuen, 1969.

Iyengar, K.R.S. *Indian Writing in English*, New Delhi: Sterling, 1985.

Kanwar, Asha S. *Ghashiram Kotwal: A Study Guide*, New Delhi: IGNOU, 1993.

——. *Feminist Theories*, New Delhi: IGNOU, 1999.

——. *The Theatre of India*. Trans. Mukherji Narayan, 2 Vols., Calcutta: Writers Workshop, 1978.

Lemon, Lee T. *A Glossary for the Study of English*, Delhi: OUP, 1974.

Levi, Sylvain. *The Theatre of India*. Trans. Mukherji Narayan, Writers Workshop, 1978.

Manchi, Sarat Babu. *Indian Drama Today*, New Delhi: Prestige, 1997.

——. *Vijay Tendulkar's Ghashiram Kotwal*, New Delhi: Asia Books, 2002.

Mee, Erin B. *Drama Contemporary*, New Delhi: OUP, 2002.

Morner, Kathleen and Rauch, Ralph. *NTC's Dictionary of Literary Terms*, New Delhi: Viva, 1998.

Nadkarni, Dnyaneshwar. *New Directions in the Marathi Theatre*, New Delhi: Maharashtra Information Centre, 1961.

Naik, M.K. *A History of Indian English Literature*, New Delhi: Sahitya Akademi, 1982.

——. *Dimensions of Indian English Literature*, New Delhi: Sterling, 1984.

——. *Studies in Indian English Literature*, New Delhi: Sterling, 1987.

Naipaul, V.S. *India: A Wounded Civilization*, London: Penguin, 1979.

——. *India: A Million Mutinies, Now*, London: Penguin, 1995.

Pandey, Sudhakar and Taraporwala, Freya eds. *The Studies in Contemporary Indian Drama*, New Delhi: Prestige, 1990.

——. *New Directions in Indian Drama*, New Delhi: Prestige, 1994.

——. *G.B. Shaw, A Critical Response,* New Delhi: Prestige, 1992.

Rangacharya, Adya. *Introduction to Bharata's Natyasastra,* Bombay, Popular Prakashan, 1966.

——. *The Indian Theatre,* New Delhi: Sahitya Akademi, 1971.

Reddy, Bayapa P. *Studies in Indian Writing in English with a Focus on Indian English Drama,* New Delhi: Prestige, 1990.

Reddy, Venkata K. *Critical Studies in Commonwealth Literature,* New Delhi: Prestige, 1994.

Schanzer, Ernest. *The Problem Plays of Shakespeare,* London: Routledge and Kegan Paul, 1963.

Sharma, Vinod Bala, ed. *Critical Perspectives: Ghashiram Kotwal,* New Delhi: Asia, 2001.

Shipley, Joseph J. *Dictionary of World Literary Terms*, New Delhi: Doaba House, 1993.

Sircar, Badal. *The Third Theatre,* Calcutta: Sircar, 1978.

Tillyard, E.M.W. *Shakespeare's Problem Plays,* Chatto and Windus, 1950.

Vatsyaya, Kapila. *Traditional Indian Theatre: Multiple Streams,* New Delhi: National Book Trust, 1980.

Williams, Raymond. *Drama from Ibsen to Eliot*, London: Chatto, 1952.

DISSERTATIONS, ARTICLES, INTERVIEWS, AND INTRODUCTIONS: ENGLISH

Bandyopadhyay, Samik. Introduction, *Ghashiram Kotwal,* by Vijay Tendulkar, Trans. Jayant Karve and Eleanor Zelliot, Calcutta: Seagull Books, 1986, iii-ix.

Banerjee, Arundhati. Introduction, *Five Plays of Vijay Tendulkar,* Bombay: OUP, 1992.

Bhatta, Krishna S. "Indo-Anglian Drama: A Critical Study", *Triveni,* 52.3, 1983, 67-73.

——. "Epic Themes in Indo-English Plays", *Triveni,* 49.4, 1981, 43-51.

—— "Indian English Drama: Models and Techniques", *Triveni,* 56.2, 1987, 31-35.

Chari, Jaganmohan and Renuka, E. "The Plays of Vijay Tendulkar", *New Quest,* Jan.-Feb., 1988, 27-28.

Deshpande, L.S. *The Limits of Translatability,* A Ph.D. Dissertation, Marathwada University, Aurangabad, 1991.

Dubey, Satyadev and Tendulkar, Vijay. "Dialogue", *Gentleman,* Sept., 1983.

Hemadri, Usha. "The Relevance of Experimental Theatre", *Indian Post,* 2 Jul., 1989, 6.

Ketkar, Kumar. "Tendulkar's Human Zoo", *The Illustrated Weekly,* 20 Nov., 1983, 22.

Marulasiddappa, K. "Drama's Turning Point", Trans., Chaitanya, *Spectrum,* 11 Jun., 1994, iv.

Moses, Sudha. *Anger and Commitment in the Post-War British Drama,* A Ph.D. Dissertation, Marathwada University, Aurangabad, 1970.

Paul, Rajinder. "Modern Indian Theatre", *Seminar,* 359, 1989, 39-42.

Pramila Devi, P. "The Theatre of Violence: A Study of Vijay Tendulkar's Plays." A Dissertation, Sri Krishnadevaraya University, 1993.

Renuka, E. "All about Umbugland: A Study of Vijay Tendulkar's Plays", A Dissertation, Kakatiya University, 1984.

Samant, Nitin. "Tendulkar: A Confused Perspective", *Adhikar Raksha* Vi, 1-2, 1983.

Sonalkar, Sudhir. "Vijay Tendulkar and Metaphor of Violence", *The Illustrated Weekly,* 20 Nov., 1983.

Sundaraman, M.N. "Tradition and Modernity in Indian English Drama", *The Journal of Indian Writing in English,* 21.1, 1993, 1-13.

Tendulkar, Vijay. *Collected Plays in Translation,* Introduction, Samik Bandyopadhyay (Introduction), New Delhi: OUP, 2002.

——. Interview by Priya Adarkar, *Enact,* 49-50, 1971.

——. Interview, *India Today,* 16-3, 1 Dec., 1980.

——. *The Indian Express,* 27 Mar., 1983, Magazine Sec., 5.

——. Interview, *The Week,* 8-14, May, 1983.

——. "Conversation", *On Looker,* 8-22, June, 1983.

——. "I Portray Women as I See Them...", *Femina,* 8-22, Jun., 1984.

Wasi, Jehanara. "New Trial in Marathi Theatre", *Link,* 1 Oct., 1989, 36.

BOOKS: MARATHI

Barve, Chandrashekhar. *Tendulkaranchi Natake,* Pune: Rajhans Prakashan, 1985.

Bhawalkar, Tara. *Marathi Natak—Nawya Disha Navi Walne,* Pune: Mehta Books, 1997.

Deshpande, D.V. *Mala Disaleli Natake,* Raviraj Books, 1989.

Deshpande, V.B. *Natyakosh,* Pune: Nishant Prakashan, Dec., 2000.

——. *Natyaspandane,* Pune: Signet Books, Shaniwarpeth, 1996.

Dhnogade, Ramesh. *Tendulkaranche Natak, Pathya wa Prayog,* Pune: Dilipraj Prakashan, 1979.

Rangacharya, Adya. *Bhartiya Rangabhoomi,* Mumbai: National Book Trust, 1990.

CRITICAL ARTICLES AND INTERVIEWS: MARATHI

Asolkar, Sharad. "Astitwawad ani Sartre", *Yugwani,* ed. Sharad Kolarkar, Nagpur: Vidharba Sahitya, 1980.

Dahake, Vasant. "Krauryanatya ani *Gidhade*", *Satyakatha,* Sept., 1975, 12-13.

Deshpande, G.P. "Shantata! Court Chalu Ahe: Kahi Vichar", *Satyakatha,* 1972, 23.

Dube, Satyadeo. "Shantata! Tendulkar Chalu Ahet", *Natyabhoomi,* 1969, 17.

Gokhale, Sharad. An Interview with Nilu Phule, *Kesari,* Sunday, May, 7, 1972, 11.

Kulkarni, G.M. "Natakkar Vijay Tendulkar: Ek Jinkane, Harne", *Satyakatha,* Dec., 1971, 38.

Lagu, Shriram. "*Gidhade*, Censorship ani Mee", *Sadhana*, Diwali Special, ed. Narendra Dabholkar, 2001, 55.

Luktuke, Ulhas. "Abhar! Rangachya Ewadhya Tukadyasathi", *Kesari*, 29 Mar., 1970, 9.

Palshikar, Vasant. *Sakharam Binder*, *Pratishthan*, May, 1973, 11-17.

All Internet Entries are from the Following Websites

http//en.wikipedia.org/wiki/vijay-tendulkar

www.indb.com/name/

http.languageindia.com/ang2007/gulatitendulkar

http.hinduonnet.com

http//salamtheatre.org/kamala2004.html

www.seraja.com

http//www.vijay.com/tendulkar

www.variety.com/www.curtainup.com/sakharambinder

www.vedamsbooks.com

www.rajanlyer.blogspot.com/2008/02/ghashiram-kotwal

http//passionforcinema.com/a-conversation-with-sir-vijay-tendulkar

www.ndtv.com/ent/booksexclusive.asp

http://www.meadev.nic.in/culture/theatre/modern.htm

http://www.meadev.nic.in/culture/literature/marathi.htm#vijay

www.rediff.com/news/dec/23vijay.htm

http://www.hinduonnet.com/thehindu/2001/09/16/stories/1416288.htm

http://www.chennaionline.com/eevents/sakharam.asp

http://www.expressindia.com/ie/daily/19991020/ile20071.html

INDEX